SHAPED BY
IMAGES

One who Presides

William Seth Adams

Church Hymnal Corporation, New York

The Church Hymnal Corporation
445 Fifth Avenue
New York, New York 10016

Publisher's note:
The author's personal editorial preference
was followed in places throughout this text.

Contents

Design & Photography   Bob Kinney

Page 11 Photograph   Rick Williams

Preface

In January, 1988, I led a retreat for the clergy of the Episcopal Diocese of Missouri, at the invitation of the then bishop, William A. Jones, III. The retreat was sparsely but enthusiastically attended. The meditations I used for those few days are at the heart of the chapters that follow. The "images" themselves were offered as food for meditation. If the intent of this book is to be understood rightly, this genesis needs to be kept in mind. This should signal to the reader that these images and their exploration were first of all to be attended by silence and reflection. They were offered such that the hearers were to be drawn into them, "lured" as it were into their own engagement with them. Though the form of what follows is no longer obviously meditational, that kind of quiet, reflective setting nonetheless remains their birthplace and to my mind continues to inform my exposition of them.

My concern here is to write about the formation of liturgical ministry and liturgical ministers at an admittedly abstracted and ideal level. I am hopeful, at the same time, that readers will translate for themselves these ideas into liturgical practice, as I myself have tried to do. What I want to offer has very much to do with liturgical practice and in that sense I intend it to be "practical." At the same time, I have been told often that what I imagine or dream to be possible in the life of a congregation is, in fact, *not* possible. Consequently, some may think the word "practical" a poor choice to describe what I have to offer. It may be, however, that "practical" will serve but "realistic" will not. Even if this is so, I am not daunted. Nor am I doubtful of my readers' ability to render my suggestions useful.

As my accomplice and companion in this kind of enterprise, I take the 17th century parson and poet, George Herbert. In his classic *The Country Parson*, Herbert describes the life of a village parson in both ideal terms and considerable detail. By so doing, he confesses, he intends to set out his vision in such a way that he (and others) may "have a Mark to aim at."[1] He adopts this intent, he says, because "he shoots higher that threatens the

Moon, than he that aims at a Tree."[2] My intentions in the chapters that follow are unapologetically the same.

Following the hatching of these ideas for the clergy of Missouri, I next developed some of them into one of two lectures I delivered as the Rossiter Lectures at Bexley Hall in Rochester, New York. (I graduated from Bexley in 1967, when it was the Divinity School of Kenyon College, Gambier, Ohio.) The lectures were delivered in October, 1988, on the occasion of the celebration of the retirement of Professor Robert J. Page, who in the mid-60's had taught me theology. For the Rossiter lecture, I summarized my list of images and explored in modest detail only three. But even at that, the exercise moved me into more disciplined discourse and away from the rather more episodic and "liquid" language common to meditations, at least at my hands.

I have used this lecture, delivered some years ago now, with my third year liturgy students at the beginning of their final semester of study, the semester in which their hearts and minds turn to things "practical." The GOEs have been written and it becomes time to get "real." It is to the generations of these students that this book owes its existence and to them that it is dedicated. Each year, they have encouraged me to take the ideas contained in summary form in the lecture/essay and to develop them more fully. Given their concern to be "practical" and "realistic" and my apparent inability to accomplish either for certain, I take their encouragement very seriously.

Shortly after delivering the Rossiter Lectures in Rochester, I rather confidently sent a copy of the lecture in question to a publisher commonly associated with the Episcopal Church, asking their impression of the work as the possible idea for a book-length manuscript. After waiting a rather long time for a reply, I was told, politely, that they were not interested, given the number of "practical" guides and handbooks that were beginning to appear. That they misunderstood my intent was clear, and probably my own fault. What I learned from the experience, however, has eventually stimulated the current project.

The publisher's rejection initially caused me to abandon doing something more with the ideas I had birthed. It was, however, the reaction of my students that changed my mind. Their interest in this material, and my eagerness that it be useful and stimulating to them, provided me with a new notion. I decided that doing the project (or not) was not going to be determined in advance by the interest (or not) of a publisher. Rather, I would do the best I could to generate and explore ideas, as if in a book, which, failing all else, I would "publish" (that is make available somehow) myself. Tumbling to this idea brought real liberation. This was so because, frankly and firstly, my concern in these ideas is the formation of the hearts and minds of theological students, specifically the students who pass through the Episcopal Theological Seminary of the Southwest and my tutelage. I realized that I did not need a publisher's *imprimatur* to move in this direction. (If others, practicing clergy for example, read these pages and find them stimulating or useful or challenging or annoying, that is an unexpected and gracious addition to the reactions of my primary intended readership.)

Further liberation followed as I came to see more clearly how this work and my own teaching bore on the liturgical life of the church. There is, I have decided, a reasonableness and almost a necessity that teachers and writers like myself, at least some of us, remain "abstractions," one of which I forthrightly call myself. It is the blessing of academic life that one has the freedom and permission to imagine ideals, to ferret out notions of principle which, at the time of discovery and presentation, come to light unsullied by circumstance or complication. Circumstance and complication will, of course, have their way in due time and course, but someone needs permission to articulate the ideal without suffering the instant subversive condemnation of hardened (and unsympathetic) practitioners.

Some years ago, at a meeting of the teachers of liturgy at North American Episcopal/Anglican theological schools, I was asked to talk about the role to be played by such teachers as ourselves in the overall liturgical education of clergy. Among other things, I said that I thought we ought to be *conservators* of the received tradition (viewed in the most critical light), and *provocateurs* of its most creative expression and enrichment. This vision informs the array of ideas presented here and also might serve as a guide for those inclined approvingly toward what I have to say.

What I hope for these images is that if they find a home in the imaginations of liturgical leaders, they will influence liturgical actions and choices of all sorts and kinds. The inferences or conclusions I draw, either oblique or obvious, I offer only as a beginning, hoping that the reader, persuaded of the aptness of the image, will continue and sustain the process. What I hope is that the images will "have their way" with the sympathetic reader, taking that person beyond whatever I see or suggest.

Having said that, readers will discover that each of the chapters that follows contains what in my view is "practical" stuff, ideas, insights, suggestions intended to bear directly on liturgical *practice*. The "realism" of all that follows must be assayed by others for themselves. For my part, I sincerely hope that some will find among all that follows, something of use.

For more technical "how-to" advice, readers will have to search elsewhere, into valuable sources already available. I am mindful here of Byron Stuhlmann's *The Prayer Book Rubrics Expanded* and Howard Galley's *The Ceremonies of the Eucharist*, books well known and well established. I also find the insights of Daniel Stevick's *The Crafting of Liturgy* very stimulating. In addition, if one were exploring the evolution of the role and understanding of the presider in an earlier time, a good compact source is Paul Bradshaw's *Liturgical Presidency in the Early Church*.[3]

All of the material that follows is original with this publication with one exception. Some of the material in the chapter entitled "One who Hosts" was published in a much modified form in an essay called "On Liturgical Hospitality" in *Our Heritage and Common Life*, edited by myself and Michael H. Floyd (New York: University Press of America, 1994), a *festschrift* honoring Professor Frank E. Sugeno on his retirement, by members of the faculty of the Episcopal Theological Seminary of the Southwest. (The publishers have given permission for my borrowings.)

The writing of these pages took place largely in the second floor front bedroom of a house on Cottle Lane in Edgartown, Massachusetts, on Martha's Vineyard. (Inspiration, however, occurred more often than not in the kitchen.) Funds for the rental of this fine old house and the securing of other necessities as well were provided to me through the financial assistance of the Conant Fund and the Board for Theological Education of the Episcopal Church. In addition, the Board of Trustees of the Episcopal Theological Seminary of the Southwest was kind enough to grant me sabbatical leave in order to tend this project. I am very grateful for this generous assistance and encouragement. I have also been wonderfully helped by the work of a number of careful readers who have improved, corrected and illuminated this work in its first expression.

With the upcoming school year (1994–1995), I will begin my twentieth year of teaching liturgical studies. Preparation for this work was accomplished at the hands of many good teachers, principal among whom have been Richard M. Spielmann at Bexley Hall and Horton Davies at Princeton University. I am grateful to them.

All the things I have written over these twenty years, and especially the collection of ideas contained here, have been informed most basically and most importantly by the work of Robert Hovda, whose *Strong, Loving and Wise* has been read by generations of my students in two theological schools and by me, more than once.[4] Though I dedicate this book to those students, it is Bob Hovda who is honored here.

William Seth Adams

Martha's Vineyard
Trinity Monday/Memorial Day
May 30, 1994

---

1. Edited, with an introduction by John N. Wall, Jr., preface by A.M. Allchin (New York: Paulist Press, 1981), p. 54.

2. *Ibid.*

3. Paul Bradshaw, *Liturgical Presidency in the Early Church* (Bramcote, Notts, UK: Grove, 1983); Howard E. Galley, *The Ceremonies of the Eucharist: A Guide to Celebration* (Cambridge, MA: Cowley, 1989); Daniel B. Stevick, *Crafting the Liturgy: A Guide to Preparers* (New York: Church Hymnal, 1990); and Bryon D. Stuhlman, *Prayer Book Rubrics Expanded* (New York: Church Hymnal, 1987).

4. (Washington, DC: The Liturgical Conference, 1976). It has been subsequently published by the Liturgical Press, Collegeville, MN.

INTRODUCTION

Over thirty years ago, during those verdant days when my seminary, Bexley Hall, sojourned in the vacant part of Ohio, we called it "priest-craft." A pejorative and unattractive word, then as now. "Priest-craft"— tactics without strategies, techniques, rote formalisms, outsides without insides, the public liturgical expression of rubricism, liturgy done as if a dance choreographed by accountants. "Priest-craft"—we avoided it and instead we studied history.

While we were doing that, however, a revolution of sorts was going on elsewhere. In December, 1963, the Second Vatican Council promulgated "the Constitution on the Sacred Liturgy," the first and surely the most far-reaching of all the declarations of that Council. It was spoken with authority to the Roman Church alone, but it was heard and in many ways heeded by much of western Christianity. The Constitution on the Sacred Liturgy is the most important liturgical document of this century, as future generations will doubtless testify. In it the liturgy was literally "re-visioned." The directives of the Constitution, of course, were incumbent upon only the Roman Church. For others, like Episcopalians, these requirements served more as an invitation, an invitation which many of us have accepted, to re-consider, to re-conceive a whole array of liturgical things. Included among these re-considerations is what concerns us here: the nature of liturgical leadership in the gathered community. A far cry from "priest-craft."

Further, the Constitution encouraged a process of liturgical reform of which now there are many signs. For Episcopalians, the singular sign of this ongoing process of reform and renewal is obviously the Book of Common Prayer in its current revision, 1979. As the Constitution did for the Roman Catholic Church, so the Prayer Book does for us. That is, the Book itself calls out of us continual reflection on the liturgical community and the presider's role, place and work within that community.

The process of responding to the Prayer Book's call for reflection has been undertaken by many. Some will think first of all of the continuing work of the Standing Liturgical Commission, a group whose clear mandate is to tend the continuing life of the Prayer Book to the good of the church. Others will think of teachers of liturgy in seminaries or the like, people whose life's work is rooted in the study and exploration of the liturgy. But, I would argue, more obvious and more continuous in their attention than commissions or professors are liturgy committees and clergy in parishes, those who struggle with this matter as a part of the week-to-week process of liturgical planning. It seems clear that more than anything else, the liturgical decision-making process itself, accomplished in countless parishes and missions, expresses or articulates assumptions about the nature of the liturgical community and the one who presides.

In our polity, the priest is by definition the leader of a liturgical community. This community is most often a parish or mission congregation, though surely it could take other forms. What I hope for in the following chapters is that the ideas presented here will assist in the formation of the heart/mind of the presider such that the life of the community served thereby is enhanced and made stronger in three aspects:

in its praise of God,
in its sense of its common life,
in its sense of its calling to enact and extend the Reign of God.

Now having declared this hope for these ideas, perhaps it would be well to lay out the model of liturgical leadership that informs my thinking and undergirds what follows. By "model" here I mean those components or dimensions which, in total, describe or encompass liturgical leadership. This model is to be contrasted with the one that seems to have informed previous generations, those formed under the influence of the previous editions of the Prayer Book. For these previous generations, of which I count myself, the essence of liturgical leadership, rather crassly put, was being on the right page. The eucharistic liturgy began on page 67 (in the 1928 edition) and we essentially proceeded straight ahead, needing to make no particular decisions for what followed. In those times, we knew nothing of the permissive rubric and all it implies. How things have changed, at least among the vigilant!

The model is composed of four elements. These elements are (1) the prayers and spirituality of the one who presides; (2) the planning process, a matter which includes the necessary creation and nurture of a liturgy committee and the liturgical education of that committee; (3) the preparation of persons and liturgical places, including the training of liturgical ministers; and (4) the action of presiding, the careful, joyful work within the liturgy itself. The integration of these elements—prayer, planning, preparation and presiding—is essential to the work of liturgical leadership in a parish. Let me explore each of these elements in a bit larger measure.

Prayer. The leader of a liturgical community is the leader of a community of prayer at prayer. Hence, the life of prayer of one who presides is at the heart of this work. Some find that their principal place of prayer is in solitude, in private devotions which they then bring to the gathered prayers of the church. Others, and here I count myself, find their principal place of prayer to be the gathered community, the prayers of the body of the faithful being the place from which solitary prayer takes life. In either case, it is the prayer life and spirituality of one who presides that supports that person's work of liturgical leadership. The work is diminished, hollowed-out when we presume to lead and do not ourselves pray.

Planning. Prior to the celebration of the liturgy, much work is needed, a multitude of decisions need to be made (or not) by people able to do such decision-making. The canons of the church place the liturgical life of a congregation in the hands of the priest in charge. This is the person understood to be qualified to make decisions. I want to suggest that the priest understand this responsibility as one *necessarily* shared with others, people who will participate in the liturgical decision-making in the parish. The creation and nurture of a liturgy committee is therefore of central importance as is the equipping of people to do this work. (It is also necessary to alert the gathered community to the rightfulness of congregational participation in liturgical decision-making.) It is here that the priest's abilities as teacher and theologian are most obviously put to work.[1]

At the same time, the principal teachers of liturgy are the Sunday liturgy itself and the building in which the liturgy is celebrated. These two "teachers" form the liturgical community most fully, for good or ill. Hence, good liturgy and a good liturgical environment will aid in the preparation of good liturgical decision-makers.

The process of liturgical planning is richly aided by an on-going process of liturgical education for the whole congregation. The content of the educational process itself and the imagined participants in the process at any given time would vary from place to place. However, if the liturgical community is to be mindful of itself as a liturgical community and be well formed as such, the process of education must be continuous and self critical.

Preparation. This aspect of the model intends to point to the preparation of persons and places for liturgical celebration. This would include in particular the preparation of liturgical ministers of all sorts and kinds. Of special importance, in my view, is the discovery and training of someone who might serve the parish as the master of ceremonies, someone whose gifts of personality and ability would qualify them to manage the variety of liturgical details attendant to every Sunday. This person, well qualified and well instructed, could be a considerable blessing for the presider, making it possible, perhaps, for the presider to prepare herself/himself for the liturgy.

As understood here, preparation presupposes the thorough preparation of the priest for the work of the liturgy. My experience suggests that often the priest's preparation is accomplished by reliance on habits. This reliance on habits in turn tends to limit the potential use of the Prayer Book's flexibility. Thus, priestly habits, and their limits, inadvertently limit the range of liturgical variety experienced in any given congregation. On the other hand, the more variety found in the liturgical life of a congregation, the more care the priest will need to take in preparation. Habits, at least in fine detail, will not serve. (The sign in the front of the classroom in which I most commonly teach reads, "Know Your Rites.") Taking the liturgy for granted is no substitute for knowing what one is doing!

Concern about preparation has altogether to do with serving the liturgical community. That is, the better we do the work of presiding, the less we will be an impediment or distraction to the gathered prayers of the church. And so, also, for those with other prominent liturgical roles. Preparation is not for the sake of performance (though, as we will see later, "performance" is important) but rather for the sake of the liturgical community.

Presiding. If all the other aspects of this model have found expression, then a strong substructure has been set in place to support the work of presiding, the careful, joyful work within the liturgy itself. The exposition of "presiding" in this model is the task of the chapters that follow this introduction.

So, then, the model of liturgical leadership that informs the work at hand. I hope the lineaments of this understanding will be visible as we go along.

Alongside this model of liturgical leadership lies the assumption that one who presides in a liturgical community is liturgist, liturgical theologian and teacher of the liturgy. The one who presides leads the liturgical community in its collected prayers and praises, aids that community to reflect upon the liturgical experience as an encounter with God and works to edify and educate the community as to the nature, development, power and implications of the liturgy itself. Liturgist, liturgical theologian, teacher of the liturgy . . . one who presides.

This three-sided view toward the work of one who presides expresses itself throughout this whole book. Most of what follows will appear to lead most directly into commentary on liturgical activity or decisions for the liturgy. At the same time, and as a continuous companion to the former, some of what is provided here is intended to work toward the formation of presiders as teachers and theologians. Indeed, it is basic to my own work and thinking to assume that presiding itself is a theological activity, containing and conveying embodied and enacted theological assumptions.

Throughout these chapters, I will contend against the clericalization of the liturgy. I will contend against any suggestion that the liturgy belongs to the priest. I will urge that the liturgy be done in such a way as to showforth the fact that the priest is a part of the community of celebration and that the liturgy is celebrated by the gathered community, the priest presiding. I regret, as I will say again later, that the word "celebrant" is used to identify the one who presides, as if to suggest that they were the only celebrant in the room. In point of fact, the community is the "celebrant" among whom someone presides. Please, dear reader, never loose sight of the community setting of all that follows, and should you catch me sounding otherwise, remember this notice—it tells the truth—and correct me in your reading. Robert Hovda said it rightly, the work of liturgical leadership is "utterly unintelligible in isolation."[2]

Let me speak of a bit of discouragement, so that once said, I can dispel it. As I travel about the church, I experience the liturgy variously done, as it should be. In my own experience and by the confession of others, I know that priestly attention to liturgical work, formation, planning, teaching is modest at best in most places, perhaps nonexistent in some. My students, most of whom leave the seminary with enthusiasm for liturgy and the liturgical community, find themselves in parishes in which what they have been taught is not and cannot be seen or done, either in the liturgy or in preparation for it. This sets loose discouragement in them and in me.

Beyond that, and I have spoken of this elsewhere before, it is discouraging to me that most priests, and perhaps the church in general, imagine that the years spent in seminary are the only years available for the liturgical education of clergy. Whereas continuing education is generally valued in the church and by most clergy, there is virtually no way clergy can pursue continuing liturgical education for themselves at the level of liturgical leadership. This seems to mean, then, that the seminaries are expected to provide for the church "finished products," so to say, a ridiculous idea to people like me. Given that the church has a College of Preachers, whose task it is to enhance the homiletical life of the church and its preachers, why not a College of Liturgists, whose task it would be to enhance the liturgical life of the church and the work of its liturgical leadership?

Two other matters by way of introduction and then we shall set about the images. The clergy imagined by this book are priests, those called and authorized by the church to preside in the community of the baptized. The priests imagined are priests who reside in parishes or missions (or the like) and who have responsibility within them as rectors, vicars, chaplains. I do not make space here for deacons, for what I hope are obvious reasons and not out of disregard, nor do these ideas accommodate very easily to priests who serve on staffs.[3]

Given the nature and shape of the Episcopal Church, and I mean this in the most affectionate manner, multiple priest staffs are an aberration. The liturgy, per se, needs only one priest, though a parish with an abundant liturgical life may need more than one person authorized to preside. The leadership which I imagine in the chapters that follow is most easily seen in association with the person who is also the canonical leader of the congregation. This is so because in my imagination a parish or mission is first of all a liturgical community, liturgical leadership, therefore, encompassing the others. This logic leads me to say, then, that in a parish or mission, normally constituted, there can only be one liturgical leader, even if there is more than one priest. I think this makes sense, as both a decision for the writing down of the following ideas and also for the self understanding of the church as gathered community.

I am helped in this view by that of Gordon Lathrop in his recent book *Holy Things*, to which reference will be made more than once.[4] It is his conviction that the liturgical community is the primary, though not exclusive, expression of the church, and that liturgical leadership is the primary, and almost exclusive, expression of ordained ministry. Lathrop writes, "Those who have the ministry of presiding will be continually invited to take joy in their circumscribed and yet immensely important tasks. They are to preside at baptisms, to preach Christ from the scriptures that have been read, to give thanks at table, to see to it that a collection for the poor is taken, and to reconcile the estranged to the purposes of the meeting. That is all they are to do under charge from their ritual appointment."[5]

This view of ordination seems true to me and basic to the remarks that follow. The circumscription of the priest's work to the liturgical realm, rightly understood, is hardly circumscription at all, for the works of mercy and justice of which the liturgy is the matrix and crucible are the calling of all the faithful, including one who presides. At the same time, this circumscription recognizes with real seriousness the network of ministries which ought to characterize the local church, within which one finds the ministry of presiding. Presiders will find particular companionship with church administrators, whose special ministry is congregational administration beyond liturgical leadership.

Lastly, I must say a word about bishops, and their virtual absence from consideration in the following pages. While it is true that the bishops of this church are the chief liturgical officers in their respective dioceses and are, therefore, the people to whom the church appropriately turns for liturgical insight and direction, the bishops do not, in fact, reside in an identifiable liturgical community nor do they exercise liturgical leadership as does a parish priest. Most bishops mourn this fact and most theorists, myself included, join them in their mourning. Gordon Lathrop again, writing about some ideal time and place, says, "Bishops will again be liturgical officers, presiding and preaching in the local church. They will focus their teaching role in the place of its origin: preaching in the assembly, not writing letters or speaking extraliturgical monologues. They will be deeply engaged in the baptismal process of the local church, perhaps inviting all the Christians of a community to make use of one common baptistry."[6] Bishops make virtually no appearance in what follows because this ideal is not near enough at hand.

We come now to the central question, "what shapes the work of presiding, or one who presides?" Or, to put the question a bit more strongly, the way a teacher or theorist might, "what *ought* to shape, what *ought* to inform the heart and mind of the presider?"

My way of approaching this question, as I have hinted already, is through a set of images. Each image is a point of entry into the same area, a sighting point on a common target, a different place to stand around a common field. This is important to remember because these images interlock, overlap, support each other, lean against each other. In fact, so far as I can tell, these ideas need each other in order to tell the truth. And, indeed, there are no doubt other images that have escaped my imagination.

The images are eight in all:

—one who presides
—one who keeps rituals
—one who handles and embodies symbols
—one who hosts
—one who remembers
—one who offers
—one who speaks
—one who celebrates

Perhaps the first thing to notice is that this is a set of activities, a list of things done. I am aiming at what someone *does* rather than who someone *is*, the work of the presider rather than the nature of the priesthood, though I admit that this distinction is slippery business. If we were to accept the false distinction between the physical and spiritual, I suppose we are talking about physicality but as I said, that is a false distinction, gnostic if I remember rightly, so this physicality is also spirituality. This seems right since what concerns us is liturgy enacted, embodied, incarnated, done, "whole" in a way—not liturgy as texts and rules, not even liturgy as books, but rather liturgy as a living reality in a living community.

When I first discovered these images for myself, and first suggested them in public, each of the images carried "the" as its first word, e.g., the one who presides, the one who keeps rituals, etc. As you see, now the definite articles have been removed. The reason for this surgery was the hope that by this minor change something rather significant could be signaled, that something more communal and less proprietary could be suggested by these titles. It is not my intent to transfer into the hands and heart of "the one" something which belongs to the community, but rather to say that within the community "one" presides.

---

1. As an aid in this work, Daniel Stevick's *Crafting the Liturgy*, cited earlier, is a valuable companion. It is intended as a "guide for preparers" and rests on the same premise of shared decision-making as what I am suggesting.

2. *Strong, Loving and Wise*, cited earlier, p. 9.

3. For serious and useful attention to the deacon's work in the liturgy, see Ormand Plater, *The Deacon in the Liturgy* (Boston: The National Center for the Diaconate, 1981).

4. *Holy Things: A Liturgical Theology* (Minneapolis, Minneapolis: Fortress, 1993).

5. *Ibid.*, p. 201.

6. *Ibid.*, p. 200.

ONE WHO PRESIDES

We begin, then, with the overarching image, the one which in some sense surrounds the others to follow. One who presides. It is Justin Martyr who gives us this image. Writing about the life of the church in Rome in the second century, Justin describes the common eucharistic practice of the time, at least as he knew it. He speaks about the bread and wine being brought to the one who presides within the assembly—or as it is put in a familiar English translation, "to the president of the brethren."[1] It is this person who gives voice to the community's prayers of blessing over the elements presented at the table.

(I am tantalized by the possibilities in the Greek underneath this typical translation. It might very well be, later developments left to the side, that the translation could equally well be put, "the one who presides among the brethren." This rendering treats the Greek with proper respect yet leaves open the possibility that presiding was perhaps not yet fixed permanently to a particular person but might have circulated within the community according to some rota or the expression of gifts or some such.)

One who presides. In choosing this image as the initial and primary one, we confront, first of all, the tradition in the Episcopal Church of calling this person "the Celebrant." Indeed, this is the language of the Prayer Book itself. In the rubrics introducing the Holy Eucharist, the bishop is referred to as the normative "principal celebrant" for the eucharistic liturgy, though this language inexplicably gives way almost immediately to "celebrant" as the rubrics continue. Given this tradition and the "official" language, one may rightly wonder about my choosing something else as the initial figure, especially given the fact that "one who celebrates" appears in our list of images, coming as it does, last.

I would argue very simply: the assembly itself is a gathering of celebrants, recipients of the grace of baptism, gathered to offer thanks and praise, to celebrate what God has done in Jesus Christ. Among the baptized, someone presides.[2] (Someone but not anyone, as will be clear as we go along.) It is as simple as that. In this understanding, it might make sense, *might* make sense, to speak of "principal" celebrant, but it does *not* make sense to speak as if there were one celebrant and not a whole roomful! (Here and throughout this book, I will avoid the tiresome question of the ontological vs. functional consequences of priestly ordination. However one votes on this issue, the fact remains that the priest presides.)

And, whereas the English are perfectly content to speak of the one who presides as "the president," given the political baggage attached to the term in this country, I, along with many others who write on the subject, use the term "presider" as an alternative.

One who presides. Beyond the technicalities just mentioned, what does this image convey? What must be true for the sense of this image? First of all, this image conveys the fact that this work, presiding, *requires other people;* and secondly, it compels us to see this work as *a work of service.* We shall explore these two notions and then draw some implications.

The work of presiding, by its very name, is contextual, collegial, communal. It presupposes the gathering. One can only preside when the gathering occurs and with the permission of the assembly. When the sacramental assembly gathers, one presides. And whatever one's responsibilities may be to bring about the activity of the gathering, without the consent of the community there is no work for the presider.

Writing very recently about this reciprocal relationship between presider and community, Gordon Lathrop talks of the common liturgical exchange, "The Lord be with you. And also with you." Lathrop, citing much earlier precedents, speaks of this exchange as a form of blessing within the gathered community, a blessing signalling the character of liturgical leadership. "The ancient *dominus vobiscum* dialogue is quite alive, marking the most important leadership moments of the presider in classic liturgies used still today. It is the most important word the liturgy has to say about leadership. The assembly cannot do without leadership roles. It would be silly to pretend to do so; we would just make up new ones. Powerful leadership corresponds to powerful ritual. But no leadership roles can do without the assembly; they require its blessing."[3] One who presides requires the permission, the "blessing" of the gathering.

An analogy here might be the conductor of an orchestra. No one disputes the importance of the conductor's role, but clearly the conductor's work depends on the prior existence of the assembled musicians and their willingness to respond to the leadership of the conductor. Conducting without an orchestra is simply a pantomime of gentle aerobics. The score goes mute without the reciprocity of conductor and musicians. So also the liturgy.

Another useful picture is provided by Soren Kierkegaard who, somewhere, depicts the liturgical event as if in a theater. There he sees actors, a prompter and an audience. In Kierkegaard's analogy, the actors are the people gathered, the prompter is the one who presides, the "priest" as Kierkegaard would have said it. And who is the audience? God, of course.

The good that this vision does is to place the assembled faithful at center stage, rightly as the actors. And it puts the presider in relation to them in a very helpful and insightful way. The presider is prompter, aiding and encouraging the work of the cast, but subordinate to it. That way of seeing things serves our purposes very well. At the same time, this picture puts God in a role that is rather too passive. The vitality of the church's sacraments could hardly be sustained by a God who merely watches. But even saying that, Kierkegaard's analogy has its obvious merits.

Yet another flash of insight is provided by Elaine Ramshaw in her *Ritual and Pastoral Care*. Here she writes, "the pastor's work is to midwife the labor of the people of God. She presides, leads, directs, and organizes, all to help the people of God do *their* work: the lector's reading, the assistant ministers' speaking or chanting, the whole assemblies' movement and singing and phrasing of petitions in prayer. A good presider is not one who force-feeds rubrics to people, like small helpings of dried-out tradition; a good presider is one who draws her congregation into the ancient dance with a new song."[4]

The point of these analogies is that each, in its own way, speaks of the primacy of the gathering, the primacy of the assembly, the primacy of the baptized, and illuminates the presider's role within that community.

One of the glories of the Book of Common Prayer, as with so many revisions in current use, is that these texts have sought very clearly to restore the liturgical community to the heart of the church's liturgical practice. And "restore" is clearly the proper term.

Paul Bradshaw, in describing the evolution (or perhaps devolution) of the presider's work, notes a change in understanding which he discerns about the fourth century. Beginning about that time, he sees a shift "from the notion of presiding over a rite celebrated corporately by the whole church to the idea of (the presbyter's) doing something for or on behalf of the people."[5] That's quite a shift—from corporate celebration towards clericalism. The texts in current use, more than any of their predecessors, have reversed this movement.

It is worth noting, in this regard, that in the rite for the Ordination of a Priest in the Prayer Book, the bishop charges the ordinand "to share in the administration of Holy Baptism and to share in the celebration of the mysteries of Christ's body and blood" (BCP, 1979: 531). "To share in . . ." One who presides, priest or bishop, is one among many liturgical ministers, all of whom comprise the assembly: readers, servers, musicians, provisioners (bakers and vintners) and on and on, and one who presides.

Further, it is also noteworthy to recall that the presbyter's liturgical work and everything else the presbyter does is delegated. That is, a presbyter's work is always derivative. It is delegated through the bishop and thereby by the church. Presbyters therefore are stewards, deputies, lieutenants in the technical sense of the term—placeholders, ciphers.

This being so, like the prompter and the midwife, one who presides is the servant of the gathered community. As such, then, the presbyter who presides needs to take on a style that has a diaconal hue, a style, a presence, a liturgical way of being that is rooted in mutuality and reciprocity, as well as in competence. One who presides in a way that has this diaconal texture or character will necessarily lay aside any hint of dominance or any suggestion of preeminence.

To put this another way, the presider's style should seek to showforth the signs of the Reign of God, the kingdom. Presiding in the church's liturgy is certainly an exercise of power, but it is just as certainly power exercised in the company of the One who chose to die, for the sake of the One for whom powerlessness itself was lifegiving.

Here we come to a central piece of business. One who presides in the church's liturgy convenes a gathering of the followers of Jesus, son of God, son of Mary. Indeed, the gathering of the eucharistic community is the showingforth of the Body of Christ in tangible human form. The members of the Body are reconstituted by the liturgy into what can never be shownforth so fully or with such power in any other time or manner. That one is invited and empowered to convoke such an assembly is daunting and wonderful. The event which is the liturgy, as Xavier John Seubert has said so well, "is a construction through gestures and words of a particular time and space in which the often tenuous connections between the level of life, from which we ordinarily live and function, and the comparatively excessive fullness of life can be embodied, engaged and entered into."[6] What a remarkable responsibility it is to be asked to call into being such an occasion!

There are implications to be drawn from what we have said to this point. First of all, let me say a few things around the theme of unity. The unity of the gathering and the unity of the rite are best signaled by one presider. The community's need for order is also best met by having one person preside. The distribution of liturgical responsibilities imagined in the Prayer Book does *not* include the parceling out of the presider's responsibilities. The opening acclamation, the collect of the day, the bidding of the peace, the declaration of God's forgiveness which typically precedes it, these belong to one who presides. And of course the table blessing, the Great Thanksgiving, is incumbent upon the presider, along with words of benediction, as they may be towards the end.

Robert Hovda approaches this same point even more strongly. He writes, "The presider's physical presence is an elementary sign to all in the assembly that the liturgical action is one thing, one ritual, with a beginning, a middle and an end . . . the visible presidency of the same person is a unifying element."[7] Though perhaps placing a too heavy burden on one person, I am inclined to agree with this view, but not to the exclusion of the presence of other unifying and ingathering presences.

This way of describing the presider's work also suggests that the work is continuous, "of a piece." In the unitive gathering, one presides in a continuous rite, composed of two integrative parts. The same word that is read and preached is, as Augustine said, made visible at the altar/table. This continuity suggests to me that changing clothes in the middle of the rite misrepresents this unitary event, particularly if the change of clothes teaches that one part of the rite is more important than another. (This I take to be the clear implication of donning a chasuble at the offertory.)

I have argued that the rich distribution of responsibilities in the liturgy includes particular work for the presider and that this work is work for one person in the gathered community. To my mind, this argues against concelebration, even though the Prayer Book invites and even commends it (BCP, 1979: 354).

We used to argue that concelebration showsforth the unity of the church. At some time that may have been true. Now, concelebration tends more to showforth the clericalization of the liturgy. And that in our time is false. The concentration of clergy who "have no necessary function," says Robert Hovda, are "among those superfluities which a firm, strong, clean ritual action abhors."[8] Well said!

In addition, most of the buildings in which the church celebrates its sacraments have a character to them which needs to be worked *against*, and the clericalization of the population at the table only exacerbates the hierarchical character built into many of our liturgical spaces. The whole affair seems to be more and more clerical as one moves towards the "east" end. For my part, if we want to have more people at the table in order to showforth the gathering of the liturgical community, we ought to make it people whose presence will work against the suggestion of the hierarchical nature of the event. That is, we might surround the table with people who by vesture and by their presence clearly suggest the assembly of the baptized.

To the question of the liturgical role appropriate to parish staff clergy not presiding at a given eucharist, I would say that they should either function as a deacon (or assisting priest) or join the congregation and share in the assembly's liturgical work.[9] As I said earlier on, the liturgy requires only one priest.

Several years ago, I had occasion to attend the Sunday eucharist at the Episcopal cathedral in Louisville, Kentucky. This is a building of Norman/Gothic design, like so many "real" Episcopal Churches. The east end, however, had been reordered and renovated, an altar/table having been set forward and the choir pews removed.

I was struck from the outset by the strong and modest leadership exercised by the dean, Geralyn Wolf. Even more startling (and wonderful to my mind) was what happened at the offertory. After the table had been prepared and the gifts of money presented, the entire congregation was invited to join the vested liturgical ministers around the altar. Remarkably enough, we all did! In this setting, the Dean and congregation chanted the Sursum corda and the lines that follow. And the Great Thanksgiving was offered clearly and powerfully by the gathered community, the Dean presiding. Communion was administered within and throughout the crowd about the table. For the post-communion thanksgiving, we returned to our original places. If there is to be any real concelebration, then this is the sort we should have! (I should add that I can imagine liturgical spaces which, by their design and use, would not require the congregational movement I have described here. The gathering of the community about the table would be accomplished by the physical organization of the room. The same would be true about the community gathered around the place from which reading and preaching took place.)

To conclude these particular implications, let me invoke again the diaconal imagery we used a moment ago, and invoke it now in connection with a particular aspect of liturgical space. It is obviously necessary for one who presides to be able to see the assembly and to be seen in return. At the same time, and in contrast to the views of Roman Catholic theorists, I see no justification for one who presides to occupy a highly elevated chair, on the central axis of the room. This arrangement is a vision given to the church in the Constantinian Revolution of the 4th century, a triumphant imitation of the emperor. Such a central location is certainly not the only location for seeing and being seen. More to the point, it seems hardly the proper seat for one who convenes the followers of one possessed of the humility of our gracious Lord.

All this having been said, I still want to advocate a "place" from which to preside. It is not for nothing that one who presides in a meeting, for example, is said "to chair" the proceedings, the obvious implication being that one who presides has a particular and specific *place* from which to exercise responsibility. This was clearly the assumption in the early life of the church in the creating of cathedrals, places which housed the *cathedra* upon which the bishop sat when speaking and acting officially. Authority and the exercise of responsibility "take place."[10]

From this "place" one would typically say the opening acclamation, pray the collect of the day, sit for the readings, be at the chair for the prayers of the people and the declaration of absolution. The peace would be bid at the chair and, following communion, the post-communion prayer would be led from there. In other words, the presider would be at the chair except when in procession, at the ambo or at the table (and at the font on baptismal days).

There might, of course, be exceptions to this norm but the norm ought to be the norm most of the time, the usual or ordinary practice. The presider's having a "place" not only tidies up the liturgy, it also assists the assembly in recognizing the formality and orderliness of the rite itself, gives continuity and cohesion to the complexities of the liturgy.

Yet frankly, my advocacy for "place" has mostly to do with the control this idea exercises over the movement of the priest. It imposes a modesty and reserve, a ritual restraint, if you will, upon the presider that is appropriate to the eucharistic event. If the chair itself is possessed of the proper modesty and is located appropriately, then the emplacement of the presider there will convey that same modesty.

It is perhaps here that something should be said about the role of the presider in setting the cadence or rhythm of the rite, particularly with regard to the management of the corporate silences invited in the eucharistic liturgy. I associate this "management" with the presider's having a proper "place." What I envisage here is the presider being responsible for the initiation of liturgical actions following the keeping of silences, and signaling the end of the silences by simple movements, gestures and changes of posture.

It might be, for example, that a silence was deemed appropriate following communion and preceding the post-communion thanksgiving. After everyone had been fed and the elements removed from the table, the presider would return to the presider's chair and, like the rest of the assembly, sit in silence. At the proper time, the presider would stand to initiate the final prayer. Others in the assembly would see this as their signal to adopt whatever was the typical posture in that place for common prayer and the post-communion prayer would follow. The presider's change of posture would end the silence-keeping. In this way, it seems to me, the presider can exercise the proper role of leadership in a modest and legible way, all the while allowing others to rest in the silence.

Needless to say, this manner of liturgical relationship would have to be taught and learned, by presider and assembly alike. But once learned and internalized, much good could follow.

Lastly, on this matter, I have argued for years that the first obligation the presider has to the liturgical community gathered for common prayer is liturgical trustworthiness. That is, it is only when the gathering has confidence in the leadership of the presider that the community is free to be about the business of common prayer. If the faithful are uncertain as to the preparedness of the presider, then they will be distracted and therefore not fully present in the liturgy.

To put this another way, the energy set loose in the liturgy ought not to be rooted in unease about the one who presides. There is, in my mind, a connection between being "in place" and being thought trustworthy. If one is rightly positioned, then things are set right, and the gathered community can proceed in its praise of God with proper expectation and confidence.

This point brings me back to the model of liturgical leadership I set out in the introductory chapter. There I suggested that if the work of prayer, planning and preparation were done and done well, then they would "describe the work of presiding, the careful, joyful work (of the presider) within the liturgy itself." Another way to make the same point is to say that the ideal towards which one strives, as a liturgical leader, is to be able to be "present" to the liturgy and the gathered community.

I am reminded of a cartoon I saw years ago. It shows people in a department store, standing on a platform between two escalators. One escalator is marked "up" and the other "down." Over the platform, above the heads of those standing there, hangs a sign reading "here." This is precisely where the presider should be able to stand throughout the liturgy. The liturgy expects, even requires, that the presider be "here." It is really a matter of the disposition and willingness of the heart, one that allows the presider to be in the liturgical gathering "as if" there were nothing else to do or think about. Indeed, the gathered community, in seeking liturgical trustworthiness, should be able to experience in a true and good way, as it were, "the real presence" of one who presides.

Many Episcopal churches, at least older ones, are equipped with bishop's chairs, chairs which typically go unused except during episcopal visits. Even on those occasions, however, because of their size and usual location in a distant corner, these chairs are often supplanted by smaller more portable chairs for the bishop's use during confirmations and ordinations, the "official" bishop's chair going neglected altogether.

In consultations with liturgy and building committees, I have advocated the abandonment of bishop's chairs in favor of presider's chairs. This is the place to be occupied by whoever presides in the liturgy. If the bishop presides, then the bishop would occupy that place. In the absence of the bishop, a priest would. The presider's chair might rightly be understood by all as the typical and rightful place of the bishop, in whose place the bishop's deputy (the parish priest) would sit in the bishop's absence. Rather than seeing this as a usurpation by the priest of the bishop's "place," we would be continuously reminded that the priest's authority was derivative of the bishop's. (The temptation, cynical perhaps yet unavoidable in my view, might also be to see in the "real presence" of the priest, the "real absence" of the bishop.) In any case, the "place" from which the ministry of liturgical leadership at the eucharist is exercised ought to be the same place, whether the presider is priest or bishop.

A final word about an assumption that ought to be lodged in the heart of anyone who presides in a liturgical community. That assumption is this: the liturgy belongs to the church, not to the priest. In any particular congregation, this would mean that the liturgy belonged to that community. Typically, the priest is invited into that liturgical community and asked to preside. Far too often, upon arrival the priest inappropriately undertakes to set the style and character of the community's liturgical life as if there had been none there before his or her arrival. And, admittedly, congregations tend to be accomplices in this, as they often "wait to see what Father or Mother wants to do."

There is, it seems to me, a style of leadership that expresses appropriate levels of initiative from the very beginning all the while recognizing the fact that one is *joining an ongoing and continuing pastoral and liturgical ministry* in the place to which one comes. One does not come to a new appointment in order to invent or reform the church, but rather to share in and help to shape and nurture the continuing life of Christ in that place. Given the enduring life of the congregation, the priest is a transient, and ought to know that and act accordingly.

1. "The First Apology of Justin, the Martyr," 65, in C.C. Richardson, ed. and trans., *Early Christian Fathers* (New York: Macmillan, 1975), p. 286.

2. On the relationship of baptism and ordination, see my article "Decoding the Obvious: Reflections on Baptismal Ministry" in Ruth Meyers, ed., *Liturgical Studies 1* (New York: Church Hymnal, 1994).

3. *Holy Things*, cited earlier, pp. 194–195.

4. (Philadelphia: Fortress, 1987), p. 22.

5. *Liturgical Presidency*, cited earlier, p. 27.

6. "Weaving a Pattern of Access: The Essence of Ritual," in *Worship* 63/6 (November, 1989), pp. 490–491.

7. *Strong, Loving and Wise*, cited earlier, p. 67.

8. *Ibid.*, p. ix.

9. For another opinion, see Howard E. Galley, *The Ceremonies of the Eucharist* (Cambridge, MA: Cowley, 1989), p. 24.

10. This is the message of a fine and stimulating book by Jonathan Z. Smith, *To Take Place: Toward a Theory of Ritual* (Chicago: University of Chicago Press, 1987).

ONE WHO KEEPS RITUALS

In a collection of essays entitled *Anglican Spirituality*, Harvey Guthrie writes about three kinds or types of ecclesiologies.[1] The first he calls confessional, Christians who organize themselves around firm and clear statements of doctrine—Lutherans gathered around the Augsburg Confession being perhaps the best case in point. The second typology is one ordered around a common and necessary religious experience. Pentecostal Christians exemplify those whose bond is fixed in this way. Particular activities associated with the Holy Spirit are expected and become characteristic of membership.

The third type in Guthrie's set he calls the pragmatic. Anglicans are his example here. These are people, Christians, who are gathered together by what they do. And it will not surprise anyone at all that he tells us that what Anglicans do is "go to church." It is not on the basis of a common set of beliefs as if a confession nor is it in a common or necessary level of religious experience, ecstatic or otherwise, that Anglicans understand themselves. Rather it is in the pragmatics of going to church together and accommodating the vast array of theological dispositions and religious experiences that Anglican ecclesiology finally expresses itself.[2]

I find Guthrie's description apt. Consequently, if for no other reason, the keeper of the church's ritual is at the very heart of our sense of ourselves. Some readers will perhaps have read Stephen Sykes book, *The Integrity of Anglicanism*, a rather contentious sort of book, in which Sykes suggests that it is the rubric-makers who have the real authority in Anglicanism. Those who are given the power and the freedom and the encouragement to revise the liturgy and to craft rubrics are the people who are in authority.[3] There is truth in this, adding all the more to the importance and centrality of the work of the ritual-keepers. Certainly the advent of the permissive rubric puts into the hands of liturgists power which they have not had so obviously before.

Ritual. Leonel Mitchell calls this "corporate symbolic activity."[4] For our purposes, I would add that rituals are patterns in which we expect to encounter God. Among Episcopalians, care for these patterns in the parochial setting falls into presbyteral hands.

Ritual is patterned, repetitious, conservative by nature. The patterns and repetitions, the predictability of them, allow the participants to enter into them safely, to be protected, reassured, not surprised or alienated. Ritual is also community making and very practical in that sense. It grows out of the people to whom it is common and it relates the people to each other and to the ritual in its enactment. Ritual creates community and gives identity. It is binding, group-making of its participants. Inside itself, a ritual communicates powerfully, by what is said and by what is not said, and by what is done. It is complex, layered with values and meaning. It is also typically in the rituals of a community that the ancient stories are enshrined and recapitulated, "experienced" and learned anew. In this way, the ritual life of a community bears the memory of that same community. Consequently, participation in the ritual life of a community is the most powerful way of forming the newly initiated and of perpetuating the formation of the continuing membership.

Rituals are often a mix of two textures, between which there may well be some tension. As Marianne Micks describes them, following Friedrich Nietzsche, one texture is Apollonian—law, order, discipline, rationality, calm, rest. The other texture is Dionysian, characterized by the impulse to excess, caprice, uncontrolability, intoxication.[5]

This duality is one that shows itself in many ways in ritual activity. Tom Driver, in his stimulating book *The Magic of Ritual*, explores the assorted pairs with considerable grace. Translating his insights into my terms, the pairs he sees are limit and innovation, establishment of repeatable forms and improvisation, ritual as shelter and ritual as path, ritual as mediator and ritual as matchmaker, ritual leader as priest and ritual leader as shaman.[6] Though this array would be tantalizing to explore in detail, what attracts our attention in the current context is this last pair, priest and shaman.

"Rituals," Driver says, "are performative actions."[7] That is, rituals are about transformation, change. In a very happy phrase, Driver says rituals "are more like washing machines than books. A book may be *about* washing, but the machine takes in dirty clothes and, if all goes well, transforms them into cleaner ones."[8] More like a washing machine than a book, indeed!

Now, given that the business of ritual activity is transformation, this puts the ritual leader in a very dynamic, even dangerous position. I say dangerous because the ritual leader is in some sense responsible for the liturgical interaction of the community and God, an interaction intended to accomplish gracious changes and renewal in the life of the community and the individuals who comprise it.

The images of shaman and priest represent two different sides or visions of the same activity. The shaman is the Dionysian one, the priest the Apollonian. If one understands the shaman as the more charismatic image, then it is probably true to say, given the history of the development of ordered ministry in the church, that the shamanistic, charismatic leadership style is an earlier expression than the priestly. (Paul Bradshaw makes this point rather clearly. As he puts it, ". . . eventually office triumphed over charism everywhere."[9]) As the community's ritual expression extends its life over time, the community's needs are best met by priestly activity, rather than shamanistic. The community's ritual keeper is most likely to be fashioned in the mode of Apollo.

At the same time, the priestly search for order and restraint clearly and almost predictably leads to stagnation and decay without the persistent challenge of the shaman's energy. Here it is that liturgical leadership needs the infusion of innovation and thereby reform and rebirth. In some ideal sense, the relationship between the images is not that of alternatives but rather one of reciprocity. In the simplest terms, the permissive rubrics in the Prayer Book invite the shaman's touch and imagination, for the sake of the health of the community and for the sake of the health of the rituals themselves.

Moving now to other notable characteristics, rituals are typically embedded in the rudiments of life and creation: blood, water, food and such. It would mean also birth, death, eating and sex—the rudimentary stuff of life and earth. Typically, ritual activity is associated with occasions of change and crisis, as we have said already. It is also commonly associated with the necessities of remembrance and with the natural seasons.

Consequently, it is not surprising to us that our central rituals have to do with food and water, a meal and a bath. It is also not surprising to us that our central ritual occasions have to do with the time of the year when the sun looks as if it will not come back and also with the time when it does. The historical reasons notwithstanding, this has fundamentally to do with ritual necessity.

Finally, not only do rituals have certain stuff of which they are made and occasions when they occur and a certain texture and predictable characteristics, they also have about them a pattern, especially on occasions of passage. It is a very simple pattern and it is acted out in the church's liturgy in clear outline. The pattern is one of separation, transition and reintegration. For example, on the occasion of baptism, the presbyter takes a child into her hands as the baptizing community gathers around the water. A child in the presbyter's hand is separated from the parental community; the child is washed, transformed, given back. Separation, transition, reintegration. We are quite persuaded that the child is not the same child. The child has died; the child has been born again; the child has been bathed; the child has been given back as a new person. The same pattern one could see acted out in weddings and ordinations. Separation, transition, reintegration.[10]

The moment of greatest ritual density is of course the moment of transition. At that moment, the recipient of the ritual action is set loose and not yet reattached. The recipient of the ritual action is socially unclassifiable. Some anthropologists have spoken of this moment as being "liminal," that is, a threshold experience, the occasion of being in-between, the moment when things change, when something is accomplished which cannot be accomplished in any other way.

Christian liturgy is a particular expression of human ritual activity, human religious ritualization. What is true in general therefore is true of us. Our ritual life is particular, peculiar *only* because of our claims about Jesus Christ. At the same time, it is fundamentally linked and related to the rituals of humankind.

As I have suggested already, one who presides, the ritual keeper, is in a position of considerable power, and the responsibilities of this person are quite specific. Putting these responsibilities in Anglican terms, one who presides must know the Book of Common Prayer and its companions; and secondly, must empower the liturgical ministries of others who share the rituals. Let me develop these two ideas briefly.

Firstly, to the presider, the guardian of the rituals, let me say: KNOW YOUR RITES. Knowing the Book of Common Prayer, the Book of Occasional Services, the Hymnal 1982 and the assorted aids and supplements which each of these has gathered to itself, knowing these means knowing the rubrics and the possibilities. Know your rites.

Our ritual activity, what we do in church, makes the church. Please believe this. Our ritual activity forms, creates, shapes, molds, brings into being the church. In our rituals, the church *expresses* itself and in our rituals the church *impresses* itself back upon itself. In what we do and say, we *express* what we believe and what we believe is *impressed* back upon us. The reciprosity of expression and impression is built into our ritual life. When we say what we believe, we are aided in our believing. When we do what we believe, we are strengthened in our believing. Expression and impression.

Consequently, it is easy to see that the richer our ritual life the more richly and fully formed is the church. I take this to mean that exercising the flexibility inherent in the Prayer Book works to the fuller, richer formation of the community of the baptized.

The Great Thanksgiving is perhaps the primary liturgical repository of our collected theology, and so it has been from the beginning. The reason Rite II has multiple eucharistic prayers is so that the varied use of these texts will not only glorify God all the more but will give fuller expression to the faith of the church. It is the use of all four over time that edifies and nurtures the church. Fixing on only one such form forever and ever abbreviates the faith of the church and truncates or diminishes the process of formation that inheres in our ritual practices.

Obviously, the same point can be made about other parts of the eucharistic rite, e.g., the content of the entrance rite or the choice of fraction anthems. Varying the ritual makes more full the form of the church.

On a related topic, it is important that the ritual keeper (and others) teach the community *the pattern* of the eucharistic liturgy. This pattern is made explicit in the Order for the Celebration of Holy Eucharist (commonly called "Rite III") but it is the same pattern for each of the eucharistic rites, it is common to them all. Indeed, it has been the pattern in the catholic tradition since the time of Justin Martyr and is now typical throughout the churches. If the eucharistic community understands that on each eucharistic occasion we gather, we read and preach, we pray and exchange the peace, we prepare the altar-table and make eucharist, we break the bread and eat—then the community will have grasped the pattern into which variety and enrichment are placed.

Communities that generate rituals and the communities generated and sustained by rituals, in ritual performance, participate in what some scholars have called "communitas," a term first provided by Victor Turner in his book, *The Ritual Process.* Turner chooses "communitas" over "community" so as "to distinguish this modality of social relationship from an 'area of common living.'"[11] In a way, what Turner is naming is the consequence of liminal experience, the consequence of having been unclassifiable, suspended from the normal conventions, "taboo" in a manner of speaking. This "suspension of the normal" sets aside the usual social conventions, expectations and norms and allows for other possibilities, other standards. Driver writes about "ritual's tendency to subordinate all privileged authority, whether derived from social structures or from spiritual life, to the overarching value of communitas, the bond of affection, or at least mutual recognition, that unites all members of the group with each other and sometimes with all other creatures in the universe."[12] In this sense, you see, the communitas associated with ritual behavior, with liminal experience, grounds its sense of order in a world *other than* that of normal social conventions. To make this point, we could use terms like eccentric, deconstructing and the like.

As I ponder what Turner and Driver offer here regarding communitas and liminality, I am reminded of the subversive nature of the Gospel and the curious promises made to us in the parables of Jesus. The Reign of God is like a mustard seed, a woman who finds a lost coin, and so on. Each and all of which I take to mean that the Reign of God simply will not be as we expect, or for that matter, hope for.

It seems important for one who presides to be mindful of this dynamic and its implications. First, perhaps, among these implications is the modesty with which one ought to take one's own place in the ritual community. One's authority rests in the community, the "communitas" of which one is a part. Further, one needs to remember that the liminality of the community "subordinates" worldly authority and celebrates the homogeneity of the community, the mutuality, the equality of all. In an important way, *each* member of the community becomes anonymous in favor of *all*, the larger, encompassing identity within which one finds oneself.

If ritual-keepers must first of all know the rites, they must also take as their mandate the empowerment of the liturgical ministries of others. If Harvey Guthrie is correct in saying that our ecclesiology is pragmatic, it is also correct to say that our ecclesiology is corporate. And it is that corporate ministry that can very well be shown forth in the church's liturgy. But it is the keeper of the ritual, one who presides, whose task it is to give it life. The liturgy invites the demonstration, the expression of this corporate ecclesiology. And when well expressed it is well impressed. What you and I know most about the liturgy of the church and the church itself, we learn in the liturgy and teach in the liturgy. The more richly exemplified the church's ministry is in the liturgy, the more well formed the church itself will be. The burden to teach and to train rests principally, though not exclusively, with one who keeps the ritual, one who presides.

In our discussion of ritual and ritual activity, it is crucial to remember that ritual activity is primarily *doing* something rather than *saying* something. And one who tends the ritual life of a community needs to be conscious of this fact. The "doing" precedes the "saying." Now, admittedly, in the old lexicon of liturgical terms, "rite" was the word for the text, the written script, and "ceremony" was the word for the things done, rubrics being the source generally. In our usage, however, we have lumped the two together, as has certainly been clear before saying so now. Yet in this blend of "rite" and "ceremony" which produces "ritual," the physical action, the "doing" takes priority, speaks first, as it were.

Let me propose two examples. First, we have the directive from Jesus which undergirds the church's eucharistic practice. As recorded in virtually every eucharistic prayer, we hear Jesus telling his table companions (whom we take to be ourselves) to "do this." The simplest and to my mind most direct reading of these words is that Jesus directs us to bless God and to eat and drink together, and that in doing so, we make his remembrance. It is, I take it, the blessing and eating and drinking which is our calling. The "saying" about Jesus's charge follows the "doing" he has required of us.

A second example appears in the Celebration and Blessing of a Marriage. At the time that the marriage is accomplished, that is at the time of the exchange of vows, the rubrics direct that the man and woman freely and obviously take and loose right hands. The man makes his vow by taking the woman's right hand and accompanies that ritual action with words. The man looses the woman's hand and she in turn takes his hand with accompanying words. They then loose hands. It is then that the priest takes the two right hands into his or her own right hand, this action declaring the accomplishment of the exchange of vows, declaring that the ritual action of promise making is complete. The priest's gesture is also accompanied by words. I would argue simply that the marriage, the promise making is done by the hands, the words functioning as a kind of descant, an overlay necessitated by custom.

Tom Driver writes, ". . . rituals are likely to bear more meaning than words can say. If we look at ritual from the front, from the point of view of its inception, we do not see clear rational meanings but instead the laying out of ways to act, prompted by felt needs, fears, joys, and aspirations."[13] Surely this is the matrix and stimulus for the ritual action of the matrimonial hands. The one who attends the rituals of the community must remember this. There is, after all, a memory maintained by the body which likely is more dependable than the memory kept in the mind. This is what prompts Nathan Mitchell to speak of the body's memory, calling it a "tactile inventory."[14] In a beautiful turn of phrase, Mitchell suggests that by this memory, by "the skin's recognition . . . God is known in the marrow before being known in the mind."[15]

Let me add a word of mild counterpoint to what I have been saying here about the priority of action, ahead of words. Though I am persuaded of the truth of this claim, I am also aware that there are some actions whose true meaning, true depth and reality are completed or made plain or consummated in words. I know of lovers, for example, whose physical expression of love preceded the speaking of it and although there was confidence in both parties that their love was true and good, it was the eventual speaking of that love that brought a settled heart.

I can imagine an argument on this wise regarding the words and actions of the marriage rite. Perhaps, some would say, the words explicate the actions, rather than merely accompany them, more than "necessitated by custom" as I said. Even this line of thinking, however, does not reduce the place and priority of the actions, it simply accords to the words a higher standing. I am content if the reader accepts and acts out this priority, giving the words whatever respect the ritual requires.

The point and the plea here is clear and simple. To take rituals seriously is to take bodies seriously. So it must be for one who keeps rituals.

I want to conclude these reflections with the consideration of something that extends the conventional limits of the ritual life of a community and some comments on what I will call "ritual criticism." If one takes seriously the importance and power of ritual activity in human communal life, and admits, as I have suggested, that some things can be best accomplished (or only accomplished) by their ritualization, then it is easy to imagine situations in which something requires ritualization for which the church provides no "script." In order to meet this pastoral and liturgical necessity, a ritual needs to be "discovered" and one who keeps the rituals must be alert to such occasions and sensitive to their coming-to-pass.

Two examples from life will serve to illustrate, one a more "private" and "secular" ritual, the other more "public" and intimately related to the church's pastoral liturgical options. A woman confronts the fact that her children are grown and leaving home, something expected and pleasing, in principle, but painful in fact. She admits to experiencing considerable difficulty in adjusting to an "adult" relationship with her children, finding her identity as their mother such as to overpower other forms of self-understanding. With the help of others, she fashions a rite of passage by which she intends to accomplish the passing over that is necessary. On a central household table, four candles are lighted, each intended to represent dimensions of relationship between the woman and her children. The four candles are lighted simultaneously. Two of the candles are interpreted to signal aspects of the woman's relationship with her children that are characteristic of their childhood alone; the other two candles are interpreted to signal aspects of her relationship with them which are lifelong, undiminished by time or changing familial circumstances. The text fashioned for the occasion voices this interpretation. It also expresses her recognition that she can let go of the former relationship without the loss of the latter, the recognition of the fact that her wellbeing and perhaps that of her current relationship with her grown children requires this passage. Committing herself to this transition, the candles signaling the former ties are extinguished, leaving burning only those signaling the enduring characteristics. The passing over was done, by all appearances and by her own witness.[16]

The other example has to do with an intended wedding for which all preparations had been made. Several short weeks before the date set, the groom while cycling was killed in a hit and run auto accident. Enormous grieving followed, accompanied by genuine and deep pastoral care. As the date of the wedding came near, the priest and the "bride," a woman in her early 50s, decided that the woman's grieving and her health depended on some acting out of her love for the man who had died and their intent to marry. Hence, between them, they adapted the marriage rite to such use. Then, on the morning that the wedding was to have occurred, a liturgy was celebrated which allowed the woman and her community of friends to accomplish a necessary and painful passage. In this ritual event, the woman was able to make public testimony to her love for her intended partner, and to her intent to have entered into a rite of Christian promise-making with him. She also gave witness, even to herself, of her convictions about God's intent to raise up whatever dies. The power of this ritualizing was remarkably palpable.

The point of offering these examples is simply to indicate the pastoral and liturgical necessity to which ritual responds and in which the actions and dispositions of God are enacted. (Even in the so-called "secular" example, surely God's penchant for giving life is in evidence, even though the text for the event contained no overt invitation to God to act.) Occasions for such ritualization will arise with their own authenticity for those attentive to the likelihood. And surely one who keeps rituals needs to be alert to ritual possibilities, conserving thereby, in an imaginative way, the Anglican (catholic Christian) tradition of liturgical pastoral care.

Finally, I want to say a word about what might be called "ritual criticism," playing upon Gordon Lathrop's phrase "liturgical criticism," about which something is said elsewhere in this book. In another place, I have suggested that liturgists need to be mindful of what I called their "congruence" in the church's liturgical life. By that I mean the congruence of the text (including rubrical material), ritual action, liturgical environment and the interpretive framework or teaching that surrounds the rite.[17] My assumption is that a rite (or portion thereof) can be said to be congruent when the relationship among these four elements is appropriate and consistent, when together they "tell the truth."

"Ritual criticism" would be the continuous use of these four ingredients as evaluative perspectives in the ritual life of a congregation. In the hands of a well-trained liturgy committee, the liturgical life of a congregation could be continuously explored and assessed. When things were found to be incongruent, that discovery would serve as an invitation to education and change, which, when guided by wise pastoral leadership, would work to the good of the ritual community and to the enrichment of their praise of God.[18]

1. "Anglican Spirituality: An Ethos and Some Issues" in William J. Wolf, ed., *Anglican Spirituality* (Wilton, CT: Morehouse-Barlow, 1982).

2. *Ibid.*, pp. 2ff. Guthrie's generalization would not sit well with some, especially those who would argue that a look at the Anglican past would contradict Guthrie. These would offer the Thirty-Nine Articles as a confessional focus that served for a time though its centrality waned, while others would suggest that whether Guthrie's view is true or not to our past, it *should* not be true of our present and future. See Michael H. Floyd's insightful essay, "Are the Scriptures Still Sufficient? The Concept of Biblical Authority in the Thirty-Nine Articles," in Adams and Floyd, *Our Heritage and Common Life*, cited earlier.

3. (London: Mowbrays, 1978), p. 96.)

4. *The Meaning of Ritual* (New York: Paulist, 1977), p. xi.

5. *The Future Present: The Phenomenon of Christian Worship* (New York: Seabury, 1970), pp. 24ff.

6. *The Magic of Ritual: Our Need for Liberating Rites that Transform Our Lives and Our Communities* (San Francisco: HarperCollins, 1991).

7. *Ibid.*, p. 94.

8. *Ibid.*, p. 93.

9. *Liturgical Presidency*, cited earlier, p. 13.

10. This pattern is typically associated with Arnold van Gennep whose book *Rites of Passage* first described it. Trans. Monika B. Vizedom and Gabrielle L. Caffee (Chicago: University of Chicago Press, 1960 [1908]).

11. Cited by Driver, *Magic of Ritual*, p. 161.

12. *Ibid.*, p. 163.

13. *Ibid.*, p. 92.

14. "The Amen Corner" in *Worship* 67/4 (July, 1993), p. 363.

15. *Ibid.*, p. 367.

16. Adrienne Rich, in a poem wherein she seeks to find "the right rune / to ease the hold of the past / upon the rest of my life / and ease my hold on the past" has written,

If some rite of separation
is still unaccomplished

between myself and the long-gone
tenants of this house,
between myself and my childhood,
and the childhood of my children,
it is I who have neglected
to perform the needed acts,
set water in corners, light and eucalyptus
in front of mirrors,
or merely pause and listen
to my own pulse vibrating
lightly as falling snow,
relentlessly as the rainstorm,
and hear what it has been saying.
It seems I am still waiting
for them to make some clear demand
some articulate sound or gesture,
for release to come from anywhere
but from inside myself.

"Toward the Solstice," in *The Dream of a Common Language, Poems 1974—1977* (New York: Norton, 1978), p. 70.

17. "Decoding the Obvious," cited earlier. In addition to "congruence," which has to do with any particular rite, I also discuss "coherence," meaning the character of the relationship between or among rites.

18. In the essay cited in the previous note, I go through this process of exploration with regard to the baptismal liturgy.

ONE WHO HANDLES
& EMBODIES SYMBOLS

One who deals with symbols is obviously a sibling of the guardian of ritual. If the ritual-keeper is the more Apollonian, the orderly one, then one whose preoccupation is *things* is surely the more dangerous one, the Dionysian. Things, bodies, material, senses, color, earth, movement, stuff. One who handles and embodies symbols is truly a materialist.

Let me begin with a story by Robert Farrar Capon in his wonderful book, *The Supper of the Lamb*.[1] In a manner reminiscent of C.S. Lewis, Capon, directing his attention to the topic of things, tells the following tale: "There was a day when Satan took counsel with his chief tempters. 'What,' he asked the assembled principalities and powers, 'What are we doing to hasten the dehumanization of the human community?' One by one they reported. Formidable senior vice-presidents in charge of envy, pride, and avarice gave glowing accounts. The chiefs of the bureaus of lust and sloth read lengthy bills of particulars. Satan however was not pleased. Even the brilliant reports of the head of the war department failed to satisfy him. He listened restively to the long treatise on nuclear proliferation; he fiddled with pencils during the section on the philosophy of the brush fire war. Finally, Satan's wrath overcame him. He swept his notes from the table and leapt to his feet. 'Self-serving declarations!' he roared. 'Am I doomed to sit forever listening to idiots trying to hide incompetence behind verbiage? Has no one anything new? Are we to spend the rest of eternity minding the store as we have for a thousand years?' At this point, the youngest tempter rose. 'With your permission, my Lord,' he said, 'I have a program.' And as Satan sat down again, he launched into his proposal for an interdepartmental bureau of desubstantialization.(!) He claimed that the dehumanization of people was going so slowly because the infernal strategy had failed to cut people off from one of the chief bulwarks against their humanity. In concentrating on offenses against God and neighbor it had failed to corrupt their relationship to things. Things, the tempter declared, by their provision of unique delights and individual astonishments, constituted a continuous refreshment of the very capacities hell was at pains to abolish. As long as people dealt with real substances they would find themselves tending to remain substantial. What was needed, therefore, was a program to deprive people of things. Satan took evident interest. 'But,' he objected, 'how shall we proceed? In an affluent society people have more things than ever. Are you saying that in the midst of such abundance they simply will not notice so bizarre a plot?' 'Not quite, my Lord,' said the tempter. 'I do not mean to take anything from them physically. Instead we shall encourage them mentally to alienate themselves from reality. I propose that we contrive a systematic substitution of abstractions, diagrams, and spiritualizations for actual beings. People must be taught to see things merely as symbols—must be trained to use them for effect, and never for themselves. Above all, the door of delight must remain firmly closed . . . It will not,' he continued, 'be as difficult as it seems. People are so firmly convinced that they are materialists that they will believe anything before they suspect us of contriving their destruction by spiritualization. By way of a little insurance, however, I have taken the liberty of arranging for an army of preachers who will continue, as in the past, to thunder against them for being materialists. They will be so busy feeling delightfully wicked that nobody will notice the day when we finally cut them loose from reality altogether."[2]

Capon warns of the spiritualization of things—the prospect of becoming "solemn idolaters spiritualizing what should be loved as matter."[3] Surely a sin of great moment!

With this we reach the heart of the liturgy and the heart of the presider's work. Our sacraments and our rituals are embodied, earthly, earthy. And whereas it is certainly true as William Temple has taught us that the universe itself is sacramental and that things do indeed bear meaning, we must begin by valuing the things, the gestures, the colors, smells, the movements *in themselves;* that is, to value these corporeal and physical things *before* we give them meaning, to honor them *before* they fall into our hands. It is after all on the basis of this value and this honor that we build, on the basis of which we understand and teach. If grace perfects nature, then we must first value nature.

Gordon Lathrop has spoken about the fact that in the liturgy, the gathering is "to set these symbolic objects in motion, to weave them together in a pattern of meaning," and I surely agree.[4] It's just that prior to setting them loose, the things themselves *as things* have value, reality, power.

What is at stake here is a willingness to admit the priority and goodness of creation in advance of any utility to us. The first creation story in Genesis bears this testimony. It is also the conviction that typically sets ecological concerns apart from other issues of common policy. To whatever use we may put them and with whatever meaning these "things" may be described, the doctrine of creation affords them value beforehand.

This line of reasoning leads me to a series of observations, beginning, perhaps strangely, with the physicality of the presider. I want to value very highly the corporeal being of one who presides, and to expect and require of that person a comparable degree of honor. Those who preside should think of themselves most of all and first of all as people for whom a body is an asset, a gift, an instrument, to be trained, exercised, taught, disciplined, enjoyed. Perhaps the analogy here is the dancer.

It is not, I think, common for us to think of liturgical leadership, presiding, as a disciplined physical activity, yet surely it is. Stylized dress, formal patterns of movement and metaphorical forms of language all signal this fact. As David Power says, ". . . the language of liturgy fits into the genus of the poetic."[5] And in this "language," most richly understood, the poetics are articulated by the whole body.

So, then, I want to consider something about the poetics of presiding. We begin with bowing. What is bowing about? Many will no doubt have watched people in church bowing, including presiders, who appear to think that bowing is dependent upon sticking one's fanny out in the air. But of course proper bowing has nothing to do with the posterior. It has altogether to do with the eyes. Bowing is an activity of the head and upper body following the eyes which are lowered. One is diverting the eyes, the body following. It is a posture of trust and respect; it is an activity of humility; in diverting the eyes, bowing is not watchful, it is trusting. The consequence of bowing is the exposure of the back of the neck—clearly a risky business. And if one bows with hands across the chest or diaphragm, then it is surely a most trusting gesture, eyes diverted, the back of the neck exposed, subject to all manner of harm, bowing. Humility, respect, trust, obedience are all the consequences of lowering the eyes and letting the body follow. One risks unbalance, insecurity, the prospect of falling. Bowing is powerful, beautiful.

In the same way consider the hands of the one who presides. Frequently I have suggested to students that the primary reason that the presider stands at the altar with hands uplifted is so that one who presides knows where his or her hands are at all times. As if to say, "it's 10:00 on Sunday morning, the Eucharist is underway, do you know where your hands are?" We know that hands left unattended will do bizarre things. They will wander off, touch, scratch, meander. Hence, keeping the hands either clearly visible or touching one another seems the most prudent course of action. (If "touching one another," one should certainly avoid "the figleaf," a posture attractive to bodyguards and other males apparently unsure about the continuing safety of their genitals!)

Further as regards the hands of one who presides, consider the power inherent in the permission those hands have from the church to touch people. Anointing, washing, feeding, healing, forgiving. This is not only permitted, it is, wonder of wonders, invited in the rubrics. What an extra-ordinary and frightening thing . . . touching people, for God's sake.

Given this power and extraordinary invitation, it seems well for the presider to recognize that this touching may be invasive, unexpected, un-wanted. In a society committed to violence, such as ours, it is necessary and sorrowing to remember that many people find being touched a source of discomfort and even horror. One who touches powerfully, as one does in ritual, needs to be mindful of this dark reality and act accordingly. This would mean, at the very least, that one would be circumspect about ritual touching and not indiscriminate or, to overstate things, promiscuous. Rit-ual restraint, about which we have spoken earlier and will speak again, is an absolute necessity for one who presides. The graciousness of touch needs thoughtful discipline.

Turning now to another aspect of the symbolic role of the presider's body, we look at the presider's presence at the altar, during the great prayer of blessing. The posture of the presider at the altar is the posture of the ancient Roman *pietas*, the figure of serenity and order, a figure that sug-gested that things were as they ought to be, at least in the Roman world. And though initially a domestic figure, she came to represent that sense of order and serenity in the world at large. Indeed, she became a common burial monument for those who in their lives had exhibited that sense of serenity and peace.

That posture lies embedded in our tradition. We associate it with the posture of Jesus on the Cross. He stretched out his arms. But prior to its being the posture of sacrifice it is the posture of innocence and vulnerabil-ity. If deflecting the eyes and exposing the back of the neck is a trusting thing, so also is exposing the breast, to stand with open hands. Open hands are non-violent hands. They plead and they praise.

All of this is to signal the fact that the posture, bearing and movement of the one who presides bear meaning, probably more than the presider knows.

We now turn our attention slightly. Typically, in our eucharistic theol-ogy, movement and gesture are accompanied by words. We have spoken about this earlier. The sign of the cross in absolution or benediction is escorted and perhaps explained or amplified by words. There are however occasions in which the rite invites or proposes gestures in silence.

It is important to note the extent to which silence is a part of the eucharistic liturgy. Occasions of silence in the past have almost invariably occurred as the consequence of error. Someone forgot something, missed a cue, fell asleep. Our current revision however invites us to be silent together, a new experience for many.

The two gestures which commend themselves to occupy a silence, or to put it differently, gestures which could stand as themselves, are a solemn bow after the Great Thanksgiving and the breaking of the bread at the Fraction.

The Fraction is a particularly powerful moment in the liturgy, although the way it is enacted in some places obscures the fact. The rubrics at the Fraction require two things: one is the breaking of the bread and the other is silence. Sadly, it is rare that this is all we do. The breaking and the silence are a combination rooted in the story of the incident on the Emmaus Road where Jesus was known to his traveling companions in the breaking. (Lk 24:13ff.) He was not known to them in anything that happened up to then, all the verbiage, the storytelling, the elbow nudging, the walk in the dust. It was the breaking. Now we have given the breaking a heavy theological overlay but surely the breaking of bread that Jesus did at the table on the Emmaus Road was in order that he might share the bread with his friends. That is, the breaking was practical, necessary. It was Jesus who fed them, not a mysterious mystical someone. It was the disposition to bless, to share, to feed, the physical act of breaking which made recognizable the presence of the One who had risen. Perhaps we have catechetical work remaining to give us "eyes to see" in this ritual breaking, at the hands of one who presides.

If there needs to be authenticity in the presider's actions and movements, there needs also to be authenticity in the things themselves. Real bread, real wine, real oil, real water.

It seems almost foolish to say "real water" but it appears necessary to do so. Water as both sign and agent in our baptismal liturgy needs to be sufficiently abundant and available to carry the symbolic weight that we want it to bear. In the baptismal rite, there is a wonderful prayer which is said in relation to the water itself. It is a prayer about water. The prayer suggests wetness, moisture, dampness, rivers, oceans, lakes, rain, bathtubs, puddles, sinks; in short, water. Ironically, oftentimes this prayer is said in the virtual absence of water. The scene is all too familiar. The candy dish approach to Christian initiation almost certainly guarantees the trivialization of this profound sign of burial and birth and bath.

The rubrics invite us at the beginning of this prayer to pour the water. It is common practice many places for the water to be already in the font, sometimes warmed ahead of time, to lessen its impact I suppose. But what of the wateriness of this outward and visible sign? Surely the water must be poured, from as high as one can reach, so that the water in its vitality is clearly seen and evident and available.

Now the consequence of pouring water from a height is that it will splash. It is just one of the things you get with water! That is likely to mean that the people standing near the water when it splashes are going to get wet. But getting wet is the point, right?!

In addition the rubrics invite one who presides to bless the water. Explicitly the rubrics say to touch the water. In my experience this touching is often done by putting a hand into the font (into which the people cannot see), and in the font the hand does something mysterious, it dabbles, does figure eights, whatever. If instead the presider were to take water in her hand and lift it up out of the font and let it run back, to splash it, it would surely make its wateriness more powerfully alive.

The point is, without the wateriness of water our talk of death and birth and bath is simply gibberish, nonsense, empty. The wateriness of baptism is the point and the concealment, the suppression of the water empties out the activity of God.

I am mindful here of the weight and authority that symbols claim in our liturgy and how their power to evoke varies depending on one's sensibilities and orientation towards them. There is obviously a necessary level of engagement of the tradition in order for one to grasp whatever may be the most superficial, didactic level of understanding. But even before engagement with the tradition, there is the necessary human capacity or willingness to let symbols speak for themselves. Further, if one were to be of the mind that symbols were "merely" some pale alternative for reality, the caustic words of Aidan Kavanaugh are pertinent: "One who is convinced that symbols and reality are mutually exclusive should avoid the liturgy. Such a one should also avoid poetry, concerts and the theater, language, loving another person, and most other attempts at communicating with one's kind. Symbol is reality at its most intense degree of being expressed. One resorts to symbol when reality swamps all other forms of discourse. This happens regularly when one approaches God with others, as in the liturgy. Symbol is thus as native to liturgy as metaphor is to language. One learns to live with symbol and metaphor or gives up the ability to speak or to worship communally."[6]

We have not labored over the traditional distinction between sign and symbol and frankly need not. But in order for me to make another point, I recount, with David Power's help, the distinction made by St. Augustine centuries ago. The distinction between sign and symbol is this: sign "'leads to knowledge of something other than itself,'" whereas symbols "make present the things that they signify and thus allow communion with them."[7] We can see this distinction readily enough and admit the currency of it in our own time and experience. We can also easily admit that the liturgy is redolent with many signs and many but perhaps fewer symbols. Now given the power of each, it seems palpably obvious that one who handles them must do so with enormous care and respect, acknowledging thereby one's own subservience to both sign and symbol, regardless of whether the thing points or effects. If communion is to be accomplished, it inheres in the things themselves and God's gracious activity in and through them. That is the source of power, not in one who handles them. In the face of such power, one acts with awe and circumspection.

We turn now to another consideration. Given the fact that symbols (and signs) are the stuff out of which ritual, language, embodiment are made, it seems incumbent upon one whose "business" is symbols to assist the gathered community in its ability to discern in them "reality." They are, after all, given to us by the God of creation who makes of them signs, symbols and instruments of salvation.

Nearly ten years ago, Margaret R. Miles published a stimulating and en-couraging book called *Image as Insight*. In it she explores what she calls "visual theology," that is theology that is made available through visual rather than verbal means. Early on she asks the provocative question, "How does eyesight become insight?" [8] This question is provoked by the fact that "the training of both eye and mind is fundamental to the quickening of religious sensibility." [9]

Professor Miles's invitation to the training of the eye is what I am after, and what I believe is required of one who handles and embodies symbols. In the simplest terms, this training would begin by encouraging the faithful assembled to watch, observe, look at what is going on around them.

Over too many years, Episcopal clergy have taught the baptized to "follow along in the book." Long after the words have been internalized and set to memory, people continue with their faces in the book. Dutifully observed, this dictum means that much liturgical action goes on unseen. In my own experience, as I have hinted earlier, the most obvious example here is the fraction. This powerful act of sharing and participation takes place without notice in most churches across the land, as do any number of others because the people in the pews are "following along." In point of fact, if they were *truly* "following along" they would be looking at the action and not at the printed page! As Miles says later on, the neglect of visual images is "the neglect of contemplation," which signals the closing off of a primary means of liturgical participation.

Consequently, the first step in training the eyes is the obvious one: people must look in order to see.

Seeing real bread and wine, real oil, real water, real embodiment and ritual action could set in motion, more powerfully than words, both attraction and association, qualities true to genuine poetics.

For example, during the action of receiving communion, how might we describe what there is to see? Following an invitation to come and eat and drink, virtually everyone in the room moves to a common place in order to be fed. Receiving in like kinds and equal portions, all return to their seats, equal beneficiaries of the gifts of the table. With eyes attuned to justice, we see here something suggestive of the Reign of God, a time and place where all are invited to eat, welcomed at the table, given equal portion with indifference as to personal characteristics; a time and place where social consideration marks the occasion, where physical accommodation is exercised as appropriate and necessary, where kindness and generosity are the overarching graces.

Surely this "seeing" into the ritual action, this discernment of the symbols of our faith, attracts us to possibilities beyond words. Surely here we "see" the allure of the gospel drawing us in. Further, in this "seeing" we might well recognize the fact that any meal could be this meal, that these possibilities remain sadly concealed but vitally present in any meal. Surely, this discernment lets us "see" the coincidence of what Monica Hellwig has named "the eucharist and the hunger of the world."[10]

"Seeing" actions of communal care and justice, gestures of humility and respect, postures of serenity and *enacting them*—this seems crucial to the reconstitution of the visual (and the physical) as means of liturgical formation for discipleship.

Tom Driver, in a book to which reference has already been made, makes a point useful to the current discussion. To "seeing," as I have described it, Driver adds "being seen." For the one who presides, and other ritual actors, both are important.

(For years, I have resisted the word "performance" in relation to the liturgy, or at least treated it as a bad word. Driver, however, successfully redeems it, to my mind, and adds a necessary dimension to our thinking.)

The "performance" of ritual activity is Driver's way of describing "the doing of it." In this sense, if we say that the whole eucharistic community celebrates together, then it would be true to say that the eucharistic community accomplishes the "performance" of this ritual meal, handling and acknowledging the signs and symbols pertinent to the action. Further, and here is where his point intersects our concerns in this chapter, he points out that in ritual action there is the "doing" and the "showing," the doing and the being seen.[11] Performance then is composed of doing and showing, both of which are necessary and integral to the efficacy of the ritual within the ritual community. And the "seeing" about which we have been speaking is the inseparable companion to "being seen." People need to be taught to "see" and the actions must be done ("shown," "performed") so as to be "seen."

With this thought we return to a topic touched on above, that is, contemplation. In a thoughtful but little-known essay, Mary Collins, O.S.B., has written about what she calls "contemplative participation," an idea suggestive of a whole range of understandings about "seeing" and liturgical participation.

Collins writes, "Contemplatives are attentive to presence." [12] It is her conviction that liturgical participation and the ability to "see" deeply into that participation are formative and expressive of a profound faith. Liturgical experience, cumulative over time, illuminated by "eyes to see," enables the liturgical community to move "from self-conscious activity to contemplative participation, rooted in experience of divine grace." [13] If this is true, then it calls all the more upon those charged with leadership in liturgical communities to enable the community "to see" and to be thoughtful about what is shown forth.

The vision that Mary Collins holds up for us is one in which the community of the baptized, a community *including* the presider, comes more and more to recognize "its own spiritual authority," thereby becoming more and more the true Body of Christ. [14] It is a community that has seen and known something holy, together.

To the notion of "seeing," in the expanded sense in which we are using the word here, Xavier John Seubert adds an essential dimension, namely, the importance of expectation. [15] For our purposes, I would put the matter this way. What is "seen" or rather "seeable" depends on the expectations of the "see-er." This is not to say that we see what we expect to see—that our seeing *causes* predictable outcomes—but rather that our expectations inform our ability to see deeply. If we do not expect deeply, we will likely not see deeply. If we do not seek efficacy, we will not likely experience it; if we do not expect vitality, we will not be disappointed. Without this necessary combination, ritual intention and symbolic power are thwarted, frustrated, neutralized.

When this happens, when this incapacity is evident, as Seubert says so well, debilitating and enfeebling things happen. "A community which is not ushered by its ceremonies into a more intense experience of its meaning center," he writes, "is cut off from its nourishment. Its contact with that which calls it into, and sustains it in being, diminishes. The community is denied approach to the transcendent which has formulated this group of people into existence as an expression and embodiment of the transcendent's power to heal and save."[16] In addition, then, to assisting the faithful to see, one who embodies symbols must also assist the faithful in their expectations.

It is important to admit, you see, that there is a sense in which the particular work of one who handles and embodies symbols is assisting the gathered community, including oneself in "discerning the body." I intend the ambiguity implicit in that statement, just as I think Paul did in 1 Cor 11:29. Be it our own materiality, our acknowledgement of community or our true expression as the Body of Christ, we are all there to be "seen."

We have discussed the necessity of full and authentic symbols—"real bread, real wine, real water"—their formative power to those with "eyes to see," and the necessity of "seeing" and "being seen." In the midst of this combination of ideas it is of first importance to remember that the symbols upon which we depend to fashion and shape, even to "make" the church, exist not finally for the church at all. As Gordon Lathrop puts it, "The recovery in local assemblies of the full signs and the clear presence of the significance of the signs is for the sake of our communication of Christian meaning."[17] And this communication is rightly called "evangelism" and is directed not to ourselves as the church, though we surely need continual renewal, but rather toward the world. In the midst of our praise of God and our celebration of redemption, the liturgy in sign and gesture, in word and symbol is fashioning vessels for the work of the gospel in the world. As symbol bearers of the Risen One, we look outward, showing-forth what we have "seen," intending and empowered to enact in the world signs of God's Reign.

---

1. (New York: Harcourt Brace Jovanovich, 1967, 1969).

2. *Ibid.*, pp. 110ff., language altered.

3. *Ibid.*, p. 115.

4. *Holy Things*, cited earlier, pp. 88–89.

5. *Unsearchable Riches: The Symbolic Nature of Liturgy* (New York: Pueblo, 1984), p. 21.

6. *Elements of Rite: A Handbook of Liturgical Style* (New York: Pueblo, 1982), p. 103.

7. *Unsearchable Riches*, cited earlier, p. 61.

8. *Image as Insight: Visual Understanding in Western Christianity and Secular Culture* (Boston: Beacon Press, 1985), p. 3.

9. *Ibid.*, p. 4.

10. *The Eucharist and the Hunger of the World* (New York: Paulist, 1976).

11. *The Magic of Ritual*, cited earlier, p. 107.

12. "Contemplative Participation" in *Contemplative Participation* (Collegeville, MN: The Liturgical Press, 1990), p. 82.

13. *Ibid.*, p. 83.

14. *Ibid.*, p. 84.

15. "Ritual Embodiment" in *Worship* 63/5 (September, 1989), pp. 402–416.

16. *Ibid.*, p. 411.

17. *Holy Things*, cited earlier, p. 173.

ONE WHO HOSTS

For years, I have valued the culinary/theological work of Robert Capon. His *Supper of the Lamb*, to which we have already referred, has been a frequent gift of mine to others and I have, myself, been the recipient of more than one of his other volumes treating matters of hospitality.

In his *Party Spirit*, the author invites us to consider "host" as an idea and as a kind of work or responsibility.[1] His observations are useful companions to things I want to say later. I should add that I set these observations alongside the comment of another, who rightly says, "God is the host of public worship," knowing that for some there may be in this combination of ideas an apparent contradiction.[2] I would only say that insofar as the liturgical assembly is seen to have a visible host, that host is the one who presides, perhaps best understood as a sign, echo, mirror, souvenir, icon, reminiscence, instrument or somesuch, of God's hospitable action. In any case, the presider's work as host and the assembly's responsibilities naturally exist in a kind of symbiotic relationship. (I remind myself and my readers of the language of Hymn 305/306 in the Hymnal 1982, "Come, risen Lord, and deign to be our guest; nay, let us be thy guest; the feast is thine.")

Returning to Robert Capon, he suggests that the simplest meaning of "host," that of provider or shelterer, "sets forth the primary obligations of the party-giver: food sufficient, drink abundant and some better ground than a street corner on which to reckon with them."[3] Further adding to this the image of "host" as an army, sallying forth, and, by extension, the "heavenly court of the Lord of Hosts himself," Capon goes on to say, "The giver of a party . . . is called to more than mere provision. He must have within him not only the resoluteness of an earthly host but the accomplished joy of the heavenly one."[4]

To these initial dimensions, Capon adds even more rich ones, the scientific and the theological. The scientific meaning, of course, holds the notion that the host is fed upon and thereby sustains others; and the theological, closely related, holds that the host is "the offered victim of a sacrifice." He writes, ". . . the host unprepared to be drained personally as well as financially is a host simply unprepared . . . This seems extreme, I know. But on any but the most trivial view of a party, it is exactly right. The labor of love to which a host goes cannot be confined to the slicing and dicing he does in advance, nor even to the actual service of his guests when they arrive. What he really owes them as a result of his sovereign call to company is his undivided attention. And to them, not simply to their needs."[5]

Translating Capon's observations from the domestic to the liturgical setting is easy enough, though obviously the one does not exhaust the meaning of the other. And caution must be expressed about isolating the presider (as "host") from the assembly (as if "guests"). I do eagerly admit the mutuality which resides at the very heart of the work of the liturgy, but surely the same might be said for the finest parties.

So, the host, one who presides. From this image a number of topics arise for our consideration, first among which is the matter of justice.

In any discussion of the liturgy, matters of justice necessarily arise early. The relationship of the church's call to corporate prayer and the church's call to acts of justice and mercy is an intimate and compelling one. The Reign of God for which we pray is the Reign of God for which we work and struggle.[6]

Typically, when liturgy and justice are discussed, the issue is treated by relating the theology and language/actions of the liturgy to issues arising "in the world," that is, outside the liturgy itself. There is, however, another way to engage the matter, supplementary to the first. This second way is to look at the relationship of liturgy and justice *within* the liturgy, thereby acknowledging that even within the liturgy the ugly head of injustice can show itself.

Looked at this way, two topics come readily to mind. The first is the liturgical use of language which is hurtful, careless, disregarding of people, exclusive. This is obviously offensive to the intent of the liturgy to re-member one corpus, to bring into being the one Body of Christ by the invocation of God's Spirit. Language that does not gather up is unjust and should be rooted out.

A second obvious example of liturgical injustice is liturgical spaces which contain physical or visual barriers to any member of the Body. If a liturgical space is to be hospitable it must be hospitable to all who would use it, and in our context, inhospitality is injustice.

So, to the extent that the host has some responsibility for the setting and ambiance for "the party," then matters of justice of these kinds fall to the host to address. This is not to suggest that the host is the only hos-pitable one, indeed the opposite is clearly the case, but to the extent that canonical responsibility locates the worship life of the congregation in the hands of the priest, then such matters of liturgical justice fall readily into those same hands.

Another justice issue needs attention here and that is the church's re-sponsibility to be hospitable to all, especially to the stranger. As with the topic of liturgy and justice, so also with hospitality to strangers, there are valuable resources which will be known already to the reader, particularly Patrick Keifert's *Welcoming the Stranger* and Parker Palmer's *The Company of Strangers*.[7] What I wish to raise is a small, some might say oblique matter related to the work of these writers.

Briefly, what Keifert, following Palmer, suggests is that in the church's search (inappropriate search, he would say) for intimacy, it risks sacrificing the possibility of public action, action clearly based on the assumption that such action is typically undertaken by strangers. Further, he suggests that it is not necessary for people to be intimates in order to do public work, like the liturgy for example. For the stranger to be welcome, intimacy cannot be a prerequisite.

This implies that the presider, in the public liturgy of the church, would always act and speak as if he or she were the host to a group of strangers. This is not to propose some sort of cold anonymity but rather a style that is (1) public, with the touch of formality that typifies this sort of action, (2) solemn, in the sense proposed by Daniel Stevick some years ago,[8] (3) corporate, recognizing that "personal" is a corporate quality, and (4) free of "codes" known only to the resident population.

There is a practice which has gained some currency in the Episcopal Church, and elsewhere I suspect, that needs attention in this connection. Given the public, personal character of the liturgy, as against a texture that might be described as intimate and private, the yearning on the part of some priests to name the recipient of the bread and/or wine seems singularly out of place. And I say this for two reasons. First of all, if one takes seriously the expected presence of strangers at any given liturgical event, then the naming of those "known" surely isolates those "unknown," and "naming" them as "friend," "brother" or "sister" only intensifies the problem (injustice?). Baptism is the rite for naming; eucharist is about something else.

Secondly and equally important, is the subversion of this rite of sacramental feeding into a moment of private intimacy between the priest and the communicant. In this sacramental action it is *not* the priest with whom the recipient is in communion, but rather the True Host, the Risen and Glorified One. To place oneself inappropriately into this communion is to become, one's own self, an idol, an interference to the true communion which all the faithful seek, even we ourselves.

Years ago, I wrote an article arguing against the use of the traditional words of administration ("The Body of our Lord Jesus Christ which was given for thee . . . ," "The Blood of our Lord Jesus Christ which was shed for thee . . .") on the grounds that the saving action of Jesus was undertaken of some collective like "all" or "the many" and not for "you, singular." The point I wanted to make was that it was our membership in that collective which availed Christ's saving gift to us. Christ did *not* die for *me* but rather for *us* (admitting that we can argue about who "us" is). If we are to use some words like those contained in the traditional administration sen-

tences, then it ought to say something to the effect that Christ died for the many, thus "you"—one of the many—take this and eat it.[9]

Given this view, the attachment of an individual name to the traditional sentences would seriously compound the lie—what I called it in the afore-mentioned essay. Here, in these current remarks, I am trying to go even further and argue against the practice of naming without regard to the sen-tence preceding the name. Leave naming to the baptismal liturgy and to times of social conversation.

Another way to speak about this last point is to recall one clear reality characteristic of the host's calling. Capon speaks about the host's "sacri-fice." I would speak about the host's "selflessness." The host's principal in-tent is the success of the gathering, the joy of the party, the well-being of the partygoers. It is not the host's own good that is the issue but rather the good of those assembled. Enhancing the engagement of those in atten-dance with each other is surely of central importance, and aiding the party-goers to know something of joy, festivity, satiety, fellowship and thereby to know the core of life, all this is supremely more important than the en-hancement of host's own self. Whatever may accrue to the good of the host's reputation, the good host's selflessness precludes seeking out mo-ments of aggrandizement. The party and the hosting thereof are for the good of the gathering, and not otherwise.

It is in this sense as well that I would argue against the intrusion of pri-vate intimacies (like naming) into the public liturgy. It does not serve to the good of the assembly.

Naming the recipient of the sacramental bread or wine risks injustice to the stranger, on the one hand, and, on the other, the making of the ad-ministrator into an idol, risks surely to be avoided.

We move now to two other matters related to the work of hosting the liturgical community. The first has to do with the issue of precedence and the second with decorum.

The eucharistic liturgy and its physical setting are filled with images and metaphors, some more powerful than others. Among the most power-ful is the meal, an easy companion to the metaphor we have just explored, the party. It is common enough for us to speak of the eucharist as a meal and the altar as a table. The heart of this metaphor rests on the fact that whereas "eating" is about food, "meal" is a social reality more about folks than food. I am quick to admit that good food is a great social help, but not so important as a good mix of people. A meal can survive poor food but not poor company.

In our context here, to take the eucharist as a meal is to take the presider as host. This would be the logic. This being so, it seems odd to me, given our cultural assumptions about hosting a meal, that the rubrics say the following: "The ministers receive the Sacrament in both kinds, and then immediately deliver it to the people" (BCP, 1979: 365); and "While the people are coming forward to receive Communion, the celebrant receives the Sacrament in both kinds. The bishops, priests, and deacons at the Holy Table then communicate, and after them the people" (BCP, 1979: 407).

". . . and after them the people." In what other social setting would the host eat first? I can think of none. Surely the norm is quite the opposite. Following on Robert Capon's testimony, it seems obvious that the host's first responsibility would be to see that all in attendance ate and drank well, after which then the host (and others sharing that responsibility) might eat. The host would not eat first and then invite the others to join, but would rather first distribute the food with care to others in hopes that all would have ample portion. Then, when all were cared for, the host would be fed.

The rubrical directives in the Prayer Book remain consistent with the received tradition, a tradition seemingly rooted in the hierarchical precedence rather than hospitality. Reading this precedence this way, the rubrics seem to suggest that the communion is properly the priest's communion, into which the people are invited to join. By this reading, should the people's invitation to receive be taken as evidence of priestly "generosity"? I can think of no other reading.

(I should perhaps mention in passing that when I have raised this concern in conversation, others have provided alternate explanations and interpretations. One suggestion has been that the rubrics reflect the custom of table companions to wait for the host to begin eating before joining in, the company awaiting the lifting of a soup spoon or salad fork to signal permission for all to begin eating. This explanation would work if, after the eucharistic food were distributed, *we were all to eat together*. Since our custom is to eat in a rather "linear" fashion, one after another, I do not find this suggestion very compelling.)

Among the Anglican liturgical books in current use, the restrictive nature of our Prayer Book is unusual in its consistent stipulation that the presider receive communion before the people. The Alternative Services Book (1980) in the Church of England and The Book of Alternative Services (1985) in the Anglican Church of Canada make no such rigid requirement, but, at least on some occasions and in certain rites, simply direct that the presider and people are to receive the Sacrament. Would that our revision were as liberal!

For my part, following the logic I have tried to lay out, I would write the rubric such that the presider (and those assisting in the distribution of the elements) receive after all others have been fed. The sign value here would rest on the social conventions rightly attached to "the host" and to the fact that the serving role is at the heart of such work. One ordained to preside, one who is authorized to speak the Great Thanksgiving, one who wears for the community the festal garment, this person is the servant who, in human terms, hosts the liturgy. Eating last would show this forth.

Archbishop Anscar Chupungco has written extensively on the inculturation of the liturgy. In a recent work entitled *Liturgical Inculturation*, Chupungco draws directly on the experience of the Roman Catholic Church in his native Philippines. In order to explain why the *Misa ng Bayang Pilipino* (Mass of the Filipino People) directs that the priest take communion last, Chupungco says, "It is intended to express the Filipino concept and value of leadership and solicitude. To eat last is not only a sign of urbanity and social grace. Above all it represents service. Thus the host eats after the guests, because the host is expected to serve and move around. Parents take their meal after the children out of solicitude. At home a person forfeits or at least weakens his or her role as leader by taking food ahead of the others. In short, taking Communion last is, in the Filipino cultural context, an affirmation of the role of the priest as the president of the assembly."[10] This puts a different spin on the point under consideration here but comes to the same conclusion. Either as a sign of presidency or servanthood, eating last ought to be the hospitable norm.

The matter of decorum, to which we now turn, is dependent on the same eucharistic metaphor, the meal. As it seems proper for the host to eat after all have been cared for, so also it seems inhospitable for the host to consume all the "leftovers" while others merely watch. (This is a rather obvious and crude way to describe the doing of the ablutions immediately following communion.) I try to imagine a dinner party in which, as the table was being cleared, the host (and perhaps a few helpers) eats what remains on the plates and drinks from the assorted glasses the remaining wine, washes and wipes the dishes, all while the rest of us watch. Even if the onlookers are invited to sing attractive music, this still seems a curious and inhospitable activity, almost rude.

(Years ago, when my family and I visited Paris, we ate several evening meals at sidewalk cafes, all in the same general area. Remarkably enough, each night, as we were finishing our meals, a particular man, older and disheveled, appeared, going from table to table, pouring into one glass the wine that remained in the other glasses on the table. At timely intervals, he would drain the glass he carried and move on. Three nights running we observed this same rather sad but ingenious fellow. My older son dubbed him "Mr. Charisma." He comes to mind every time I observe public priestly ablutions!)

The rubrics clearly permit the consumption of whatever remains of the consecrated elements after the Dismissal, that is, after the rite is over. Surely this is a better alternative. Do the dishes later! It is also worth noting that the ablutions are not peculiarly priestly work—"the celebrant or deacon, and other communicants, reverently eat and drink [whatever remains]" (BCP, 1979: 409)—even though the public, ceremonial doing of them would clearly suggest the opposite. The domestic practice is the best teacher here. Either do the dishes later or, as a happy alternative, invite *everyone* to stay after and help.

Further, consider the subtle social message contained in the action of the priest at the altar/table consuming the remains of the wine. Watching the priest stand at the altar/table and drink the remaining wine seems to dignify the abundant consumption of alcohol in an inappropriate way. Certainly an addictive culture like ours does not need more such examples to fuel its dependencies.

In some places, the "space" in the liturgy created by the public doing of ablutions has attracted the attention of parish musicians, who have seen this as a time for special congregational or choir music. My suggestion of removing the ablutions to another time (outside the liturgy) has elicited from some a mourning of the loss of that time for music. My response is to suggest that if the music is appropriate on its own terms, then it might be left there, and that after the remaining elements have been removed from the altar/table to the credence table, the presider go back to the presider's chair, adopt whatever is the proper posture and enjoy the music, or sing along, or do whatever is liturgically sensible. The point is simply that doing the ablutions within the liturgy itself is not necessary and certainly not edifying—nor, is it hospitable.

I want to turn now to what some might call, in a negative way, "control." What I mean here is that it is the host's responsibility to know and sustain the mood or texture of the liturgical occasion. That any given liturgical event has a proper texture or feel is undeniable. The calendar obviously gives thematic texture and the rites of passage contained in the Prayer Book clearly necessitate continuous sensitivity to the way the theological and liturgical substance of the rite express themselves. The host, perhaps with the aid of others, will help to determine this texture and the way it is expressed and experienced.

In previous chapters, we talked about the tension that resides in the liturgy between order and intoxication, rest and excitement, Apollo and Dionysus. There is one moment in the Sunday liturgy in many parishes where this tension is too often allowed to be broken. This particular moment is the exchange of the peace.

In the earlier years of textual revision, most parish priests, at least those who thought that "the peace" was a good thing, worked hard at encouraging the faithful to greet one another in Christ's name. For some reason, in some places, perhaps due to the influence of the style of informal, small group eucharists or some frustrated need for (public) intimacy, this formal, eschatological greeting has gotten out of hand and, essentially, broken loose from the rest of the liturgy. The ritual restraint that rightly characterizes the liturgy as a whole is abandoned, being replaced by something quite intrusive and ritually inappropriate. The balance achieved by the healthy tension between Apollo and Dionysus has given way and the "chummi-ness" of a class reunion makes its appearance in the midst of the liturgy.

In addition, in my experience, it is very common for some people to greet some neighbors in one manner and others in quite a different way, as if some neighbors were "preferred." The "preferred" neighbor gets the grander greeting. Strangers are alerted to their place. Though they may be the neighbor the Lord provided, they are *not* the neighbor of choice. The liturgy has none of this in mind.

I raise this issue in this particular chapter because I believe that it is the presider's responsibility to assist the congregation to express the proper texture of the rite, to know and value ritual restraint. The presider's teaching *and example* are of basic importance here. By dint of training and sensibilities, the presider must know the proper level of ritual engagement and teach it and demonstrate it. The more persuaded of the public, corporate, ceremonial nature of presiding, the more clear this responsibility will be.

I want to conclude this chapter with some reflections on one other activity characteristic of one who hosts. Though what I am about to say is exceptionable, it is nonetheless typical of the host to be one who blesses, one who says grace before the meal.

In the eucharistic context, this is to call attention to the canonical fact that the blessing of things and people is reserved to priests (and bishops). The logic here, though not commonly expressed in this way so far as I know, must be rooted in the assumption that the presbyter, following the Greek, is an *elder*, and it is common enough in various ethnic and religious communities for the elders to be those known to be possessed of the gift of blessing. (This logic is tested, of course, when, as was my case in one of the parishes I served right out of seminary, the "elder" [me] is 27 years old and the youngest active member of the congregation is 64!)

Another way of looking at this, of course, would be to say that the priest's responsibility to bless or authority to bless or ability to bless *in the name of the church* is a consequence of the spiritual grace of ordination. I say "in the name of the church" recognizing that people bless others all the time and in many and varied ways. In our polity, however, and for the sake of order, we authorize priests and ask God to empower them to speak words of blessing. And we bring to such blessings confidence that in those words and actions, what is said is accomplished, that something of God's divine intention is disclosed and effected.

I have said in a number of ordination sermons what I believe to be true, namely that the authority exercised by the priest is the godly authority of the church, authority which the church by the grace of God empowers the priest to exercise. When the church ordains a priest, the church knowingly expects to receive and experience the benefits of the authority bestowed and the grace conveyed, as if to see the ordination, as with baptisms, as God's commitment to sustain the church into some future. All of which is to say that the authority exercised by the priest belongs to the church *and not to the priest*.

The priest's speaking and enacting the Great Thanksgiving, then, is not something done either "instead of" or "on behalf of" anyone. Rather, the priest voices the great prayer of thanks within and among those on the basis of whose authority the priest is privileged to speak and act. The efficacy of the prayer rests in God's disposition to faithfulness, the keeping of promises made to the church and the graces given the church to their fulfillment. (My hunch is that the language of "on behalf of" derives from a time when central liturgical and sacramental activity took place in the absence of the rest of the ritual community. In their absence, surrogacy became a way of explaining how it was that the absent were active in the rite. This logic would hold true for understanding the High Priesthood of the ancient Temple or the sacramental priesthood of the rising Middle Ages. For our time and place, it is more accurate and faithful to say that the priest speaks and acts *among* those present rather than "on behalf of" the absent.)

What this suggests is that, whereas by the normal social conventions the host of a party might imagine that the convening of the party is by the action of the host, with the eucharistic meal things are rather different. It is, as it were, the church who convenes the party, asking and empowering the priest to act out the duties and obligations of the host. But this eventuates in the same result as with the party conventionally understood, namely, the host is servant of the party, the gathering, the assembly, the meal. So, we have come back to where we began, and perhaps as Eliot suggests, have known the place for the first time.

Let me move now to remarks about the relationship of blessing and power. Here I am informed by the writings of Janet Walton and John Baldovin.

Walton's essay, "Ecclesiastical and Feminist Blessing: Women as Objects and Subjects of the Power of Blessing," makes plain the traditional understanding and the inequities therein contained that (in human social terms) blessings are an inherent manifestation of power, the one doing the blessing being the possessor of power not possessed by the recipient. Behind this is the assumption that in the words and actions of blessing something is conveyed to the recipient from "outside" or "above," peculiar access to which is available to the one pronouncing or enacting the blessing. "Something missing" is being provided.[11]

The intent of her article is to confront the inequality implicit in this understanding and to propose a cooperative or communal understanding to supplant one rooted in dominance. My intent is the same though my strategy a bit different. In pursuit of that end, I turn to John Baldovin.[12]

Baldovin makes a distinction on which I want to rely. He describes two understandings of sacramental action, understandings associated with the action of blessing. He writes, "In one approach the sacraments are channels of grace from God to a fundamentally ungraced world. They are vehicles of God's condescending mercy by which the faith of the church and of individuals within it is strengthened. In another view, however, sacramental activity arises out of the world that has already received God's self-communication or grace. There sacraments act not, as it were, from above but from within the world and the church as the sacrament of the world's salvation." He elaborates this second understanding this way: "Liturgy or sacramental activity 'works' not so much by transferring a grace [understood as some kind of quality] to those who do not have it as by enlivening or, if you wish, fermenting the grace-filled faith that exists in the baptized."[13]

It is this second understanding that I want to appropriate and associate with the host's work and action of blessing. And I want to use it to interpret or better reinterpret Professor Walton's concern.

I take Baldovin (and Karl Rahner behind him) to be giving a very high place indeed to God's act of creation, in which there inheres already a blessing. Sacramental activity (and acts of blessing in general) undertake to "ferment" or set in motion what already exists, by God's grace. If this is so, one negative aspect of the power question is neutralized. We are not in the importation business, epiclesises not withstanding!

Secondly, and returning to a point made earlier about the host's role within the community as the one who says the blessing at the eucharist, if the priest is empowered by the prayers of the church and the grace of the Spirit to pronounce the church's blessing, then the power exercised is the power "possessed" by the church, not by the priest. The priest is not functioning "on behalf of" the powerless. "Rather," as Baldovin says, "[the eucharist and the eucharistic blessing are] the self-expression of the Body of Christ, head and members, made visible in a ritual manner."[14]

It is important for one who hosts the ritual community to understand deeply the power exercised by right (rite) of ordination. If it is clearly and passionately held as the godly power of the church, then a proper modesty will necessarily accompany its expression.

In this chapter we have spent a good deal of time with the meal metaphor for the eucharistic event. A word or two about domestic meals and matters of justice will serve as an appropriate conclusion to our observations in this section.

In many households, the only time the family sits together on a regular basis is at mealtimes. No other times seem available. If there is tension or unhappiness in the family, it often shows itself over meals, the only real opportunity for its expression. For some, this fact leaves a taint on meals (and family life) such that it is difficult to remove. In some cases, the family chooses to disguise the unhappiness in the family—at mealtimes—in such a way as to create a more harmonious tone (read "the appearance of harmony") rather than to engage or experience the unhappiness with an eye to resolution. I have described this as choosing harmony (the appearance of same) over justice (the resolution of things). This is a choice that must not be made at the eucharistic table. The harmony that is to characterize the community which gathers at the eucharistic table must be harmony rooted in justice.

I would take this further. Whereas in some households table conversation is restricted to "agreeable" topics only, at the eucharistic table things "agreeable" to conversation are without limit. To this table one can bring sorrows, sins, anger, tears, happiness, uncertainty, fullness, nakedness of any sort. (As Auden says, "That we, too, may come to the picnic with nothing to hide . . ."[15]) The justice of the eucharistic table lives in this freedom. The hypocrisy of choosing harmony over justice has no proper place at the sacramental table, where we are all, as Dan Stevick calls us, "debtors to grace" and possessed of common and equal value.[16] The table in the midst of the liturgy must stand in an atmosphere of safety indifferent to personal status or claim, and be surrounded by an aura of indiscriminate mercy and conspicuous justice.

One who hosts such a gathering will know that the liturgy creates and enacts, at its best and most ripe, what Robert Hovda once called "a Kingdom scene" in which we see and know God's provision of "refreshment."[17] Such is the true nature of Christian hospitality.

---

1. *Party Spirit: Some Entertaining Principles* (New York: William Morrow, 1979). Capon excuses his persistent use of male pronouns and since he does, I must regrettably do likewise.

2. Patrick Keifert, *Welcoming the Stranger: A Public Theology of Worship and Evangelism* (Minneapolis, Minneapolis: Fortress, 1992), p. 58.

3. *Party Spirit*, cited earlier, p. 24.

4. *Ibid.*

5. *Ibid.*, p. 25.

6. Readers of these pages will already know important literature on this subject, among the best being *Liturgy, Justice and the Reign of God*, written by J. Frank Henderson, Kathleen Quinn and Stephen Larson (New York: Paulist, 1989).

7. Patrick Keifert, *Welcoming the Stranger: A Public Theology of Worship and Evangelism* (Minneapolis, MN: Fortress, 1992); Parker Palmer, *The Company of Strangers: Christians and the Renewal of America's Public Life* (New York: Crossroad, 1986).

8. Daniel B. Stevick, *Language in Worship: Reflections on a Crisis* (New York: Seabury, 1970). This term is explored later in these remarks, in the chapter on One who Speaks.

9. "Given and Shed for Whom?: A Study of the Words of Administration" in *The Anglican Theological Review*, LXVII/1 (January, 1985).

10. *Liturgical Inculturation: Sacramentals, Religiosity, and Catechesis* (Collegeville, MN: The Liturgical Press/Pueblo, 1992), p. 41.

11. In *Blessing and Power*, edited by Mary Collins and David Power (Edinburgh: T. & T. Clark, 1985).

12. "Liturgical Presidency: The Sacramental Question" in John F. Baldovin, SJ, *Worship: City, Church and Renewal* (Washington, DC: The Pastoral Press, 1991).

13. *Ibid.*, pp. 119–120.

14. *Ibid.*, p. 121.

15. "Horae Canonicae VI. Compline." W. H. Auden, *Selected Poems*, New Edition, edited by Edward Mendelson (New York: Vintage Books, 1979), p. 231.

16. *Crafting the Liturgy*, cited earlier, p. 60.

17. *Strong, Loving and Wise*, cited earlier, p. 20.

ONE WHO REMEMBERS

It seems ironic to me that a person like myself whose most obvious qualification for professorial work is a penchant for absentmindedness should give himself over to a discussion of remembering, but there it is. Happily, the remembering to which we want to address ourselves is not the sort that one is unable to exercise at the market (my particular affliction) but rather a related but different sort. It is the kind of remembering that is *anamnetic* and formative of community identity, rooted both in the past and present, anticipating of the future, and truthtelling.

We begin by returning to something we said earlier. When we spoke about the work of the host, we commented about the responsibility of the host to say the blessing, an activity reserved in some societies to elders. I pointed out in that context that the priest's being *presbyteros*, meaning elder, may explain in a way the entitlement the priest holds to be the community's "sayer of grace." It may well be, I suggested, that the grace of ordination transmits and accomplishes in the recipient of such grace the requisite benedictional gifts of the elder. In the current context, however, something else is required. Here what is necessary is the memory of the elder, the formation of the elder.

How is one formed as an elder, without the prerequisite blessings and agonies of age and experience? This is a solid question and one, frankly, I want to treat evasively. In a proper world, it may well be that in order to preside in a liturgical community one *ought* to be in truth and in fact an elder. Given, however, the nature of the church and the character of theological education in our time, teachers like myself must be content with the formation of (relatively) "young" elders.

The elder as remembrancer. The elder as one who tends the cultic memory, one who assists in the continuous fashioning of the community, one who helps to delineate a future by calling into the present the influence of the past. This is the subject of this chapter but to put the matter that way is nearly to mislead. In actuality, it is not really to the elder that we look for all this but rather to the liturgy itself and the liturgical community, in the midst of which stands one who presides.

It is the nature of ritual activity to be formative of the ritual community, the ritual creating and shaping the community in which the ritual is enacted. The "doing" and the "being seen" are constitutive of the community. Integral to the ritual activity is the cultic memory that is recalled and expressed and, thereby, impressed upon the participants. The identity of the ritual community is announced and instilled by the rehearsal and re-engagement of the cultic memory. As a continuous process over time, the rehearsal and re-engagement of the cultic memory sustain the life of the community into the future. Memory carries with it anticipation.

Consider the case of the amnesiac, one who is without memory. Such a person, in real existential ways, simply does not exist. No memory, no existence. People "come into existence" as they acquire something to remember about themselves. That a person cannot remember their name requires others to give them a name. Those who surround this nameless one simply cannot tolerate namelessness, that is, identity-lessness. Acquiring a name conveys the beginnings of a new memory and the beginnings of identity. Slowly, the experience that follows upon the loss of memory brings into existence someone who has really not existed before, one who comes to rely on the new memory for identity and meaning. It is only at this point, ironically, that the "new person" has a future, has the capacity to anticipate, to look forward. The creation (or restoration for that matter) of a past is prerequisite for the making of a future, as if to say, "If I don't know who I am, how do I know what to hope for!"

The liturgical community guards against this loss of identity and anticipation in vital and important ways, relying in practice on one who presides, though this is by no means work peculiar to the priest. The "guards" to which I refer are the calendar and the rehearsal and re-engagement of the cultic story, writ both large and small.

The anthropological legacy available to us at this point presents us with an interpretative struggle between those who claim a priority to the story (commonly called "myth") and those who would claim priority for the ritual, that is that "the (ritual) actions in which human beings engage cannot be reduced to some kind of surrogate for words."[1] "Rituals acquire mythical or symbolic interpretations in the course of time."[2] For our purposes, I am content to stand with David Power, who says, ". . . it can be said that memorial in Christian liturgy is constituted by both narrative ("myth") and ritual and by their interaction. The narrative serves as the means for an active remembering of Christ's mysteries and an active projection of the hope of the kingdom. The rite encompasses the community and signifies the mode of being of a people who keep this memory as a source of life and hope."[3] My digest of this is to say that the doing of the rite and the saying of the narrative ("myth") are constitutive of Christian liturgy, expressive and formative of the Christian memory and the Christian community.

As to the work of the presider, we turn first to the apostle Paul, who in 1 Corinthians 11:23 sets out a paradigmatic description of the presider's work as remembrancer (though obviously not peculiar to the presider), ". . . I received from the Lord what I also handed on to you . . ." (NRSV). The pivotal Greek words here are *paralambano* meaning "to take and join to oneself," typically translated "to receive" and *paradidomi* meaning "to give over." *Paradosis* is the word typically translated "tradition." What Paul describes then is a process, "What I have taken and joined to myself, I give over into your hands." This is the process of "traditioning," as it were. One receives first oneself and then passes the treasure along. (Here one sees the essence of the catechetical process.)

This foundational statement leads me to say that one who presides *must* be shaped and formed in the tradition, *must* be the willing recipient of the church's experience in mind and body, that is, liturgically, and *must* be able and willing to be an agent for the passing on of that tradition. At the same time, and more will be said about this later, one who presides *must* actively exercise what Gordon Lathrop calls "liturgical criticism" and *must* recognize that the vitality of the tradition depends on continuous and vigorous reinterpretation.[4] On this latter point we shall enlist the aid of Marjorie Procter-Smith.[5] For catholic Christians, the principal medium for this "traditioning" is the liturgy. In the liturgy we experience what one liturgical theologian has called "embodied remembering."[6] The pattern for our remembering is set by the keeping of the Christian calendar and the practice of the rhythm of Christian liturgical observance.

In 1982, in *Studies in Formative Spirituality*, Christopher Kiesling published an article entitled "The Formative Influence of Liturgy."[7] The insight Kiesling brings to the subject at hand has informed my thinking ever since and has been expressed in various writings of my own, his being duly credited of course. What interests Kiesling is the church's habit of keeping seasons, "whole chunks of time to which the church gives a particular meaning and mood through the liturgy."[8] The influence exerted by the keeping of the seasons, Kiesling admits is "subtle" and since it occurs over extended periods of time is pervasive and, therefore, powerful. He is keen to argue that the impact of season keeping "insofar as it is not resisted but allowed to have its way, is truly formative: that is, promotes psychological and spiritual balance and growth."[9] The "balance and growth" which Kiesling values is the "traditioning" that I intend to value.

The keeping of seasons takes the liturgical community through the story that gives us identity, provides occasions for the re-engagement of that story and for the appropriation of its content and influence. In addition to seasons, the keeping of principal festivals and the continuous reoccurrence of definitional moments and events work to the same end. (I should be quick to add that the *reason* we keep the calendar and the principal festivals is the praise of God, the enjoyment of God and *not* self-consciously the formation of the community. The formation of the community, however, is a happy and predictable consequence of this patterned corporate prayer and not to be neglected or despised.)

Marjorie Procter-Smith speaks about formation and season-keeping in a beautiful way. Writing about "embodied remembrance," she says, ". . . embodied remembrance is found at the center of all Christian liturgy insofar as that liturgy remembers, and remembering, celebrates the Paschal Mystery of Jesus Christ crucified, dead, risen, and present in the power of the Spirit. It is found generously extended and elaborated in the church year. It appears condensed and terse in the anaphora. It is recognized and hymned in rising sun and evening light in the daily office."[10]

At the center, then, of our remembering, "traditioning" and liturgical formation is the Paschal Mystery. It is its echoes, reverberations, resonances, replications that we discover and celebrate in calendar and festival. That this is so puts the ritual of the Triduum, the three day festival of Jesus' death and rising, at the absolute center of our liturgical and formational life. That is, the keeping of Good Friday, Holy Saturday and Easter in the calendar stand where death, entombment and resurrection do in our theology. The saving power and transforming energy of the death and resurrection of Jesus are recalled and set loose in the liturgy. Robert Hovda turns a fine phrase on this point. He says that the liturgical year "feeds the paschal mystery to us in pieces small enough to chew."[11]

For one who remembers, and whose responsibility it is to assist a community to remember for the sake of its identity, this means that the Easter festivals must obviously and consistently be the principal festivals of the community's life. Our culture will not assist the accomplishing of this but the obligation remains nonetheless. The Prayer Book is intent on this fact as the presence of the liturgies of Holy Week makes quite plain. It is in this week and its culmination that our cultic memory is made most intense and visceral, our rituals the most elaborate and rich, our symbols most vibrant.

It is an odd thing, however, given this fact, that the keeping of the Great Fifty Days seems so difficult. Much is made of Lent, perhaps for good reason, but the celebration of the season of Easter is, by comparison, a very pale thing. Is it perhaps because we are more ready to believe and declare our own sinfulness and need for repentance and salvation than we are ready to believe and celebrate God's willingness to be gracious to us? (I recall Dan Stevick's apt and likeable phrase, "debtors to grace.") Perhaps we are more willing to admit our debt (Lent-keeping) than to praise God for the grace given so bounteously and to revel in it (Easter-keeping). Curious.

One modest way to extend the texture of Easter Day through the season is to omit the confession from the corporate liturgy, intending thereby to suggest that for a season, we might "wallow" in the prodigality of the resurrection. Surely, if we have kept a Holy Lent, we have thereby prepared ourselves to be reasonably decent bearers of God's generosity.

We return now to something else Professor Procter-Smith points out. In the quotation cited earlier, she remarks that the Paschal Mystery occurs in a "condensed and terse" form in the Great Thanksgiving. This is certainly true. Central to this condensation, of course, is the reiteration of the story of Jesus' last meal with his closest followers.

For centuries, the narrative of the institution has been contained in the church's eucharistic prayers. The narrative has served generations of western Christian theologians as the locus or "moment" of consecration of the bread and wine. In answer to the question "when" has come the answer, "during the recitation of the narrative of the institution." Most theologians of our time have abandoned this rather particularist and mechanical view in favor of a larger, less mechanical, more communal view of the consequence of blessing.

For our purposes at the moment, however, the point I want to make has to do with the fact that in the narrative, and indeed in the whole eucharistic action at the table, we are *not* re-enacting the Last Supper, we are celebrating the church's eucharist. We are not mimicking Jesus and his disciples. (As Procter-Smith says, "*Anamnesis* is not *mimesis*."[12]) We are *not* pretending to do anything. We are doing what Jesus told us to do, in the midst of which we declare the warrant for our actions. Obviously we engage and participate in the tradition, and in this engagement we experience the *anamnetic* reality, the availability now of the lifegiving and lifesaving effects of what happened "once upon a time."

In the saying of the prayer of blessing, the Great Thanksgiving, the priest is *not* acting as if Christ. Again there is no pretence here. The rubrics that direct the priest to touch the bread and cup, perhaps to raise them, are not intending to encourage confusion about the liturgical identity of one who presides. The touching or raising have to do with calling visual, tactile attention to the things being blessed, to the action of blessing, and are *not* intended to suggest that the priest is pretending to be Jesus.[13]

At the same time, given that Jesus and his disciples were sharing a meal, a significant even festive meal, and given the fact that such events have very common currency in the human community, and that the blessing of food is typical of such occasions, there is no reason at all not to see the priest and Jesus as functioning in the same mode, that is as ones who say blessings over food in the midst of friends. This view is rather different, however, from imagining that the priest *is*, for liturgical purposes, Jesus.

The liturgy provokes and accomplishes *anamnesis*, the making present of the saving power and transforming energy of the Christ event. In the liturgy and the calendar we re-engage and recount the tradition that forms us. I have argued earlier that in the ritual life of the church the church it-self is continuously created. In this chapter, I have suggested that our cor-porate memory carries the "genetics" for who it is that we will prove to be. This being so, we need to look with care at the content of the memory we maintain, the memory that gives us identity, the "traditioning" to which we submit ourselves and which we pass on. Several topics require our at-tention in this regard.

In *Holy Things*, a book to which several references have already been made, Gordon Lathrop speaks of "liturgical criticism." As to how liturgical criticism might function and serve a local congregation, Lathrop says, "li-turgical criticism inquires about ritual meaning and symbolic strength."[14] What he is naming here is of first importance for one who remembers be-cause it is the rightful perspective for continuous and necessary review of the formative tradition, be it expressed in ritual, symbol or story.

The concern that Lathrop raises and explores is a concern that, one hopes, surfaces in the week-to-week liturgical life of a congregation, at least one in which there is thoughtful reflection on the liturgy among those charged with preparing the liturgy. It seems so obvious. Though I have never used the phrase, liturgical criticism has characterized much of my writing and teaching over the years.[15] That is, questions of the con-gruence of rite, ritual action, hermeneutic and ritual setting have been continuously important, along with the matter of the coherence of one rite with another imagined to be a compatible sibling. Does the rite "tell the truth?" Are the signs and symbols sufficient for the significance they are to carry? Is the truth claimed in words visible to the eyes? These kinds of questions and many more are available and necessary to be asked in the "traditioning process."

Taking "liturgical criticism" a step further, and with particular regard to the keeping of the calendar, one who remembers needs to remember that the ideals of the calendar are not necessarily without taint. Let me explain by example.

With the 1979 revision of the Book of Common Prayer, a fine array of liturgies was made available for the keeping of Holy Week. The availability of these texts has stimulated many congregations to a much fuller and richer observance of this powerful and central time. Indeed, if the Triduum is the heart of our liturgical memory and our theology, then the keeping of Holy Week is instrumental to the formation of a community which bears that memory and espouses that theology. The provision of the rites has surely strengthened the church.

At the same time, we need to remember that there is undeniably an anti-Semitism built into the gospel telling of the events of Jesus' last days, especially at the hands of John the Evangelist. It is not "the crowd" or "some of the people" or "those who collaborated with the Roman occupation" who are the villains; it is "the Jews." This has meant, over time, that Holy Week has been the season most productive of hate crimes against Jews.[16] Christian anti-Semitism is part of our tradition, surely a part of which we can only be ashamed, but one that risks perpetuation through the passing on of ritual words (and actions) which escape "liturgical criticism." One who remembers *must* remember the dark side as well, with an eye to its vigorous amelioration. The anamnesis which is to shape and form us must be truthtelling.

There is yet another matter which requires our attention. If it is true that "Christian liturgy requires a profound remembering, which renews and reclaims the significance of past events for the present," and if that liturgy "suffers when its memory . . . is faulty or incomplete," then it is easy to admit that under such circumstances "Christian liturgy may tend toward heresy or self-deception."[17] The logic seems irrefutable. This being so, what of the virtual absence of the memory of women in the church's calendar and liturgical tradition?

Many readers will know that this issue is cogently explored by Marjorie Procter-Smith, who is convinced, as I am, that our liturgical memory does indeed have "something missing." She writes that "the proposal to include women's memory in liturgical anamnesis is not simply a matter of adding a few women's names to the eucharistic text or increasing the number of lectionary texts which mention women. Rather, the locating of women's memory in Christian liturgical anamnesis will yield a profound reexperiencing of the entire Christian tradition."[18]

The memory which the church bears is a patriarchal memory, both in its formation and in its content. Every conventional history of the church and its liturgy attests to this fact. The awakening in our time of liberation theology, in this case as regards women but intending the liberation of all (even oppressors), raises for the church the remarkable task of fashioning a new, richer, more truthful memory.

It seems crucial to me that women's liturgical anamnesis be reconstructed and restored to the church, both for the sake of women and their life with God, and for the church. Though it will not accomplish this end directly, the use of non-gender specific language in the liturgy (and in preaching and the rest of life) will help to vanquish a serious obstacle. So long as our liturgical forms are populated by male-dominant language for the human community and its members, and exclusively masculine imagery for God, there is little likelihood that the restoration of the liturgical memory of women will come to pass. The injustice of exclusive language is clear, it seems to me, and its subtle harm insidious.

Change in language use is a powerful and significant step, since language shapes the way we see and think, and not the other way around. At the same time, restoring the memory of women to the liturgy carries with it such a challenge to the received tradition that one grieves at the prospect of failure. The risk is that the liturgical memory of women *will not be able* to find expression in the church. Given the historical and existential marginalization of women and the continued proprietorship of the liturgy by men, it would be small wonder. Perhaps, to take a more hopeful view, with the increased number of women taking places of leadership in the church and the continued freeing of the imagination of women, even fundamental changes will be able to occur within a community recognizable as the church. For myself, I remain hopeful and expectant, and eager and willing to be taught and led in what surely will be a necessary "re-experiencing" of what has come to us.

We now turn our attention to another dimension of memory maintenance. The calendar we keep and the lectionaries that attend them are constituted by several layers of observance. There is most obviously the Sunday and seasonal calendar. There is then the sometimes "seasonless" daily calendar and lectionary. Thirdly, there is the sanctoral cycle, that calendar which, in the Episcopal Church, is enshrined in the red and white letter days commemorated in the Prayer Book and those kept in *Lesser Feasts and Fasts*, a list that is regularly tended by the Standing Liturgical Commission and General Convention.

The sanctoral cycle has its own history which need not detain us here except to say that as it expresses itself in the Episcopal Church, it too has several layers. I want to argue that it should have one more.

The first layer of our sanctoral cycle is the catholic one, that layer of observance that unites us with other catholic Christians over time and space. The second layer is that peculiar to the Episcopal Church, a layer populated by people whose example is specifically important to Episcopalians in the United States. This impulse to particularity is very important, since it suggests to us, rightly, that there are godly examples of Christlike living to be found in our own national history and our own national church.

The additional layer I want to advocate for the calendar-keeping in any particular congregation is the remembrance, at least for a time, of events and persons peculiar to that particular parish or mission. This, after all, is the way the sanctoral cycle came to be in the first place.

What I am proposing (with due pastoral caution) is that in those remarkable instances of truly saintly lives and deeds, that they be remembered in a particular place for a year or two, perhaps longer, perhaps not. There are, in virtually every congregation, persons whose lives expressed something powerful and wonderful about life with Christ in community.

The life which was celebrated in the Burial Eucharist might well be remembered a year later, on the anniversary of what was once called a "birthday into eternity." This date might be kept only once, but its observance in a particular place with a particular people could nonetheless be a formative influence upon those who gather to praise God and remember. (It might well be that the custom of giving memorial altar flowers is suggestive of this somewhat larger idea.)

Throughout this chapter, it has become obvious that one who remembers must be, to some extent, a kind of liturgical raconteur, one for whom the telling (or "doing" or "dancing" or "showing") of stories is native. The absence of this gift would not likely disqualify an aspirant from ordination but the work of memory maintenance and storytelling must be done, both liturgically and extraliturgically, for the sake of the liturgical community. One who remembers needs to admit this and tend to it, either one's own self or with the active aid of others (surely a preferred alternative to heroic efforts in the first place). Particularly at the local level, raising up local storytellers who can sustain the local narrative, memory and identity is very important. And the recapitulation of those memories in the liturgy, in association with the catholic lineage into which they are woven, is a powerful nutrient of life in the church.

To conclude this chapter, I want to return to something touched on earlier, namely, the connection between the active memory of things past and the contents of an imagined future.

Our talk of the power and influence of memory carries the risk that some will think that we are concerned particularly with the past, that we are standing with our backs to the future in an effort to get the past "right." This could not be further from the truth. As we have said earlier, our concern with the past and its power has entirely to do with the present and the future, the past being the reservoir or wellspring out of which flows our present and beyond.

It is also true to say that our memory is the primary storehouse or inventory for our imagination. Whether we remember in order to avoid the past or we remember in order to duplicate it (both options are caricatures), the remembrance of things past is prerequisite to imagining a future. Taking this a step further, what we remember will either restrict or enlarge the future we see for ourselves. This is so for the obvious reason that memory is formative of identity and identity is formative of imagination. Who we understand ourselves to be informs what we imagine.

We have talked in this chapter about matters of identity and formation, and about matters of justice (the recollection of the dark side of the tradition and the reconstruction of what is missing from our memory). We have done so in order to alert one who remembers to the substance of the task and its importance. But the real issue is what the liturgical community hopes for, to what it aspires, the form its faithfulness will take by its own conviction and decision, the intentions of God the Holy Spirit notwithstanding. Remember, the Jesus whom we remember is the Jesus whom we await. The One whom we remember is the One whom we recognize now and will recognize in God's future. The shape and content of our memory, the "stuff" which our anamnesis provides to us, is the "stuff" of our hoped-for future. One who remembers must remember this.

"Now I am rampant with memory," says ninety-year-old Hagar Shipley, the central character in Margaret Laurence's wonderful novel, *The Stone Angel*.[19] "Rampant with memory." So it must also be with the followers of Jesus.

---

1. Tom Driver, *The Magic of Ritual*, cited earlier, p. 92.

2. *Ibid.*

3. *Unsearchable Riches*, cited earlier, p. 130.

4. *Holy Things*, cited earlier, chapter 7.

5. *In Her Own Rite: Constructing Feminist Liturgical Tradition* (Nashville, Nashville: Abingdon, 1990), chapter 2.

6. *Ibid.*, p. 41.

7. (III/3, November, 1982).

8. *Ibid.*, p. 378.

9. *Ibid.*, p. 378.

10. *In Her Own Rite*, cited earlier, p. 41.

11. *Strong, Loving and Wise*, cited earlier, p. 77.

12. *In Her Own Rite*, cited earlier, p. 53.

13. For an interesting excursion into the theological complexities of this view regarding the priest's functioning *in persona Christi*, one might begin with Kenneth Untener's article "Forum: The Ordination of Women: Can the Horizons Widen?" in *Worship*, 65/1 (January, 1991), pp. 50–59. This article sparked responses which extend and compound the matter at hand. See Charles R. Meyer and Sara Butler, "Forum: The Ordination of Women: Responses to Bishop Kenneth Untener" in *Worship*, 65/3 (May, 1991), pp. 256–268 and John R. Sheets, "Forum: The Ordination of Women" in *Worship*, 65/5 (September, 1991), pp. 451–461.

14. *Holy Things*, cited earlier, p. 162.

15. These comments reprise remarks made earlier, in the chapter "One who Keeps Rituals.". My term there was "ritual criticism," a term which was stimulated by an earlier reading of Lathrop.

16. See my article "Christian Liturgy, Scripture and the Jews" in *The Journal of Ecumenical Studies*, Winter, 1988.

17. Marjorie Procter-Smith, *In Her Own Rite*, cited earlier, pp. 36–37.

18. *Ibid.*, p. 39.

19. (Chicago: University of Chicago Press, 1993). Originally published in 1964.

ONE WHO OFFERS

To this point in our deliberations, the overriding and most commonly used liturgical metaphor has been the meal, the central symbol of which we have called a table. There is, however, in our eucharistic tradition another metaphor and another symbol. These are sacrifice and altar. We turn our attention to them now, admitting at the outset that they each carry a complex and challenging history and content. That we use "priest" puts sacrifice in the mix unavoidably and "sacrifice" inexorably carries along its "place." ("Offering" and "oblation" will come into play as well, though on a more modest scale.)

It is perhaps then appropriate first of all to remind ourselves of a fact often forgotten by catholic Christian clergy, clergy for whom "priest" is common coin. In the New Testament, only Jesus and the community of the church are spoken of in priestly terms. Jesus (Hebrews 4:20 and following) is our great High Priest and the community of the faithful is a "holy" and "royal" priesthood (1 Peter 2:5,9; similarly Rev 1:6 and 5:10), possessing what the Reformers called "the priesthood of all believers." Those of us subsequently called by the word "priest" are, in the Christian Scriptures, called "elders," about which we have said some things already. It is the testimony of the New Testament writers that the necessity and lineage of earthly sacrificial priesthood has come to a full stop, Jesus being the conclusion and consummate heavenly expression thereof.

Our "priest" is the vestige of the transfer of the Greek *hiereus* into the Latin *sacerdos*, and the English corruption of presbyter into priest. Recognizing this linguistic history ought to constrain present day "priests" from confusing themselves, their calling and ordinations with that of Jesus or with the true calling of the whole community of the baptized.[1] If there is sacrificing going on and if it is priestly, it is at the hands of Jesus and through participation in his sacrifice by the priestly people, of whom the ordained person is a member. By this reading, the "priest" does not offer "sacrifice." Whatever is offered is offered by the church through the risen and ascended One.

Two recent writers have made insightful observations about sacrifice and eucharist. The first is Kenneth Stevenson, who in *Accept This Offering* explores a set of five objections which some might raise about the continued use of sacrifice as a theological theme in the eucharistic context.[2]

His most potent response to objectors, in my view, is "to argue that . . . sacrifice is a powerful *metaphor* which conveys something of the power, the passion, the feeling of the Eucharist that seems to have gone out of some of our more staid, clinical celebrations. Today's world needs that metaphor . . . In a world that knows about suffering in its own way, the metaphor of sacrifice has returned, with a new and vibrant meaning . . ."[3] He says a bit later, "We need to recover the *cost* of the Eucharist in liturgy and piety for a generation that has learnt to 'have a Eucharist' in much the way that it likes to drop in for a cup of tea."[4]

To Stevenson's comments I want to add something from Gordon Lathrop. Quite bluntly, Lathrop says, "Christian worship is not sacrifice . . . at least not in a literal sense of the word. In many ways this seems an obvious assertion. No procession of the victim is held; no animals are slain in the assembly; no holy violence occurs here, there is no sacred knife or bloody stone; God is not given something to eat. Christian worship is rather a communal gathering that enacts or remembers the baptismal bath, reads and interprets scriptures, and holds the meal of bread and wine. Under no definition of sacrifice as a cultic procedure can this ritual of the Christians be regarded as included."[5]

Yet, though doubtless Lathrop is right, he like many others wants to use the word and honor its endurance in the tradition. To accomplish this, he turns for assistance to the notion that Stevenson relies on, metaphor. Lathrop says that in metaphor we intend "to use the wrong word in order to reveal to the imagination a plurality of meanings that otherwise could not be spoken . . . The wrongness of the word needs to be heightened, not tamed, in order for the figure of speech to work. We need to inquire what truth about God is proposed by our calling our assembly action sacrifice when it is not."[6] Metaphor is the self-conscious use of "the wrong word" in order to reveal more meaning. By calling what we do "sacrifice," it is evocative beyond its more constrained limits.

Between them, Stevenson and Lathrop provide us a set of textures or meanings with which to work. We add to them historical observations from Robert Daly. In *The Origin of the Christian Doctrine of Sacrifice*, Daly comes to the following conclusion: "For the New Testament church, Christian sacrifice was not a cultic but rather an ethical idea, an idea that could include prayer and worship in the formal sense, but was not constituted by them. It was centered not in a formal act of cultic or external ceremonial worship but rather in the everyday practical life of Christian virtue, of being 'for others' as Christ was 'for us.' It was a totally free and loving response, carried out on the practical level of human experience, to Christ's act of self-giving love."[7] Whereas Stevenson and Lathrop speak about Christian sacrifice associated with the eucharist as "metaphor," Daly's word is "spiritualized (=christologized)," meaning that the revelatory quality of "the wrong word" must reveal the ethical dispositions of Christ. Failure to recognize this, he says, will "call upon ourselves the stern rebuke Paul leveled against the Corinthians: 'It is not the Lord's Supper which you celebrate'" (1 Cor 11:20).[8]

From this collection of learned insights, we take permission to deal knowingly and imaginatively with "sacrifice" and its siblings, "offering" and "oblation," and we adopt a range of ideas, or better a vocabulary, to which we will return more than once. Setting out these ideas, this vocabulary, as if a painter setting out materials (and admitting that I will add others), I will use them principally for what they evoke.

It interests me, first of all, to remember that the etymology of "sacrifice" gives us "to make holy or sacred," though the dictionary's definition takes us a different direction, toward "offering," where we will go in a moment. The making holy of things/places/people, in the Christian tradition, is the consequence of God's actions, invited or invoked with particular intention. The "holy making" of sacrifice (the wrong word) carries with it the hint of bloodletting and the necessity of invocation. Robert Jensen, writing in a densely written book some years ago, said "It is universal among humankind that, second to sexual intercourse, eating together is the most binding communal act . . . [I]n religiously vital cultures, the fellowship essentially involves God; every right meal is a sacrifice. For to eat we must kill (if someone thinks that killing only plant life avoids this, he only betrays an anthropomorphism for which most of mankind has anciently been too sophisticated). To eat is to kill in order to give life. And only God can do that. Therefore, to eat is to blaspheme—unless we pray God to join the act. If we do, the meal is a sacrifice."[9] Howard Nemerov's pithy poem "Behavior" is worth calling to mind at this point:

> Among our good deeds of this date:
> Removed a turtle from the drive
> And saved a drowning butterfly.
> At evening, bowing over meat,
> We call down grace on all alive.[10]

The church's eucharist is obviously a meal, and if Jensen is right, it becomes a sacrifice rather than a blasphemy by God's action following our invocation. So, by this logic, sacrifice being "the wrong word" reveals to us something profound about the structure and content of our eucharistic praying.

To wit, for generations among western Christians it has been the narrative of the institution that has been the center of theological attention in assessing the consecratory action of the eucharistic prayer. (I confess that this has always amused and surprised me, given the fact that the recitation of the narrative does not possess the character of prayer. Calvin rightly saw it as the "warrant" for our actions but that it should necessarily find its way into the prayer formulas seems odd.) For eastern Christians, however, it has been the epiclesis that has been so honored. It is now common in western eucharist prayers for the epiclesis to have a place, either before or after the narrative. It is also fairly common for the action of God to be invoked with regard to both the people and the elements.

Following Jensen's logic, surely it ought to be the epiclesis that takes pride of place, its being the moment when blasphemy becomes sacrifice, when desecration becomes consecration, sacred-making. I am not proposing that we return to theory and actions attached to some notion of "the moment of consecration" but rather that the actions dictated by the Prayer Book to accompany the narrative be supplemented with actions appropriate to the epiclesis. At the very least, the balance of the two would convey and sustain a more full "consecratory" understanding, an understanding implicit in the combining of narrative and epiclesis in the same prayer form.

It would also follow that extraordinary liturgical gestures like genuflections or solemn bows would occur only after the accomplishment of the full prayer text, rather than, say, following or during the narrative. It is the action of the whole community and the offering of the whole eucharistic prayer (containing the combination of narrative and epiclesis) that accomplishes whatever is accomplished. A solemn bow in silence after the Great Amen seems to me a proper response to these consecratory events.

We move now to the suffering and violence that abide at the heart of any notion of sacrifice. And, in Christian theological terms, this is where we meet the Paschal Mystery, the delicate central nerve of the faith and the essence of our anamnesis.[11]

This Mystery is first of all *passion* (Power's category *Pascha/Passio*), an abhorrent magnet which has drawn the imagination of artists as often as the prayers of the faithful. "Eli, eli . . ." Jesus's voicing of the Psalmist's words sets loose in the heavens the cry of all who suffer, the brazen question shouted by all who know abandonment, war, starvation, brutality. One thinks here of Grunewald's altarpiece at Isenheim where the gnarled limbs and sagging shriveled body of Jesus showforth and summarize the horrors that resound through human life and history. Jesus the grotesque One, dying.

It is not the point here to make overmuch of crucifixion as a form of death, for surely later generations have devised more exquisite means—flaying and gas chambers come to mind. Rather it is to see, as others have, that in this particular death, by whatever means, God suffers. (How Greek theologians could imagine the *impassibility* of God and still read either the Psalms, the prophets, the Song of Songs or the passion narratives is beyond my imagination!)

If "passion" contains suffering, it also contains what we recognize in our word "passionate," a kind of fury, whether this be the fury of "crimes of passion" or the fury of the passion of physical love. If we miss this ingredient, we misunderstand the person of Jesus and again misrepresent God. In a remarkable passage, James Agee has said, "Every fury on earth has been absorbed in time, as art, or as religion, or as authority in one form or another. The deadliest blow the enemy of the human soul can strike is to do fury honor . . . Official acceptance is the one unmistakable symptom that salvation is beaten again, and is the one surest sign of fatal misunderstanding, and is the kiss of Judas."[12]

". . . to do fury honor." It seems such an easy thing for us to eviscerate the passion or to trivialize or domesticate it by missing its furious, passionate side. The Good Shepherd as eunuch! The cross, instrument of death, as jewelry or ornament!

What we recognize and warn against is the co-optation of the passionate Jesus and the according to him of a dignity of an inappropriate kind, the making of Jesus into someone "dignified." This dimension of the passion of Jesus must always keep it *eccentric* to the standards of the world, however central his person and work are to our theology.

If, then, on the one hand the Paschal Mystery has within it passion as suffering and passion as fury, it has also passage (Power's category *Pascha/Transitus*). By this we mean the passing over into God's possession. This is central to any understanding of sacrifice. The victim (or the vitality of the victim) passes over. The lifeblood that is set loose frees the life of the victim to be God's own. Our sign of passage, of passing over is the resurrection, seen first for us by the women who sought to attend the decaying body of Jesus only to discover that he had risen.

The reader will perhaps recall van Gennep's description of rites of passage as we talked about it earlier, namely, separation-transition-reintegration ("One who Keeps Rituals"). It comes to me now that this describes in a powerful and unique way the experience of Jesus in that time our liturgical lexicon calls the Triduum. And the women who met him were the first to receive him back from that most liminal of times. (We will speak in due time about our own entrance into this experience and our own engagement of this reality first known that first Easter by our foremothers.)

To this point we have treated several dimensions of the Paschal Mystery into which, we will suggest, Jesus' followers enter by their *participation* with him in this mystery. Before doing that, however, we need to explore one more dimension. To suffering, violence and passage we add surrender. If "sacrifice" has been our informing category to now, perhaps "offering" and "oblation" need to be moved into more central light.

As I call "offering" into our conversation, I want first to use the word not as with alms basins and bread and wine but rather as another name for surrender. As one thinks about sacrifice and the victim, the victim in such a situation is typically not "a volunteer" as conventionally understood. Yet in the person and example of Jesus we have a victim by surrender. He "offers" himself, as the liturgy says, as both priest and victim. The willingness of Jesus to surrender to the cross and to the will of God is crucial to any verbal or physical sign value to be attached to our "offering" anything as Christians, either within the liturgy or without.

It is only on this basis that the offering associated with alms or bread and wine is properly so-called. If our offering is not willingly surrendered, it is not imitating of Christ and therefore not a holy offering. An *oblata* given by coercion or manipulation is an unworthy one.

We mentioned earlier the technical term "participation" and promised to return to it in due time. In order to keep that promise, let me begin this way. The eucharistic texts contained in the Prayer Book come to us informed and shaped by both the history of eucharistic praying and the continuous experience of the faithful. Readers will be able to provide for themselves the substance of Reformation debates about the character of sacrifice appropriately associated with the liturgical work of the church. Whereas Luther so opposed any such association that he stripped the eucharistic prayer of everything except the institution narrative, reformers like Thomas Cranmer were much more conservative of the received tradition. While Cranmer was absolutely clear about the fact that Jesus had made "one oblation of himself once offered, a full, perfect and sufficient sacrifice, oblation and satisfaction for the sins of the whole world," he was nonetheless willing to speak of such things as the "sacrifice of praise and thanksgiving" which could be offered by the church as well as the offering and presentation of "ourselves, our souls and bodies," as "a reasonable, holy and living sacrifice."

More recent texts remain equally as convinced as Cranmer about the uniqueness of Jesus' sacrifice and, like earlier forms, connect our offering of gifts or praise and thanksgiving with *anamnesis*, that recalling which sets loose among us now the effects of Christ's death, resurrection and ascension.

Insofar as the Christian life is concerned, what is crucial in all this is our *participation* in Christ and thereby in his sacrifice. In Eucharistic Prayer B of Rite II we ask of God, "Unite us to your Son in his sacrifice, that we may be acceptable through him, being sanctified by the Holy Spirit" (BCP 1979: 369).

More than anyone else, the apostle Paul has taught us about our "participation" in Christ, what it means to be *en Christo*. It means that we are "a new creation" (2 Cor 5:17); that "all of us who have been baptized into Christ Jesus were baptized into his death" and that having been "buried with him by baptism into his death . . . we too might walk in newness of life" (Rom 6:3); that in our eucharistic eating and drinking "the cup of blessing that we bless . . . is a sharing in the blood of Christ" and "the bread that we break . . . is a sharing in the body of Christ" (1 Cor 10:16). Therefore, says Paul to the Ephesians, "be imitators of God . . . and live in love, as Christ loved us and gave himself up for us, a fragrant offering and sacrifice to God" (Eph 5:1–2).

Throughout the patristic age and beyond, these convictions of Paul's found continuing expression.[13] Throughout our history, it has been baptism that has been the occasion of our being gathered into Christ's resurrected and risen life and into the community which remains his earthly

Body. It is also baptism that gathers us into Christ's sacrifice. I take this particular aspect of our participation in Christ to mean that we share in his sacrifice both as priest and as victim.

The priesthood of Christ's sacrifice in which we participate is that to which the language of Hebrews and 1 Peter direct our attention and which is reiterated in the baptismal liturgy. After the washing and signing/sealing, we admonish the newly baptized to "share with us in his eternal priesthood" (BCP 1979: 308). The "priesthood of the church" is the shore onto which the baptized are "washed." Those of us who have already made the passage bid the new arrivals welcome.

It is on the basis of this fact and this language that those of us who preside in the liturgical community must be very leery of calling ourselves "priests" and imagining that the representation to God of Christ's eternal sacrifice is peculiarly attached to our ministrations. It is, in truth and in fact, the church itself which makes this offering, the hands and voice of which we are privileged to be, at least for a season.

As victim, our participation in Christ's sacrifice requires of us self-abandonment, a kind of "kenosis" which Paul saw so clearly in the Risen One, the one who "emptied himself" for our sake (Phil 2:5ff.). It is here that the church's "participation in Christ" has a profound impact on the life of the liturgical community. With particular reference to the issues explored in this chapter—sacrifice as holy-making, passion as suffering and fury and passing over, offering and oblation as surrender—the consequences of our liturgical language and actions, if they be truthbearing and formative of the community, must and will express themselves in acts of justice and mercy.

Taking the perspectives of priest and victim into view simultaneously, as if through a stereopticon, we focus directly on that event in the eucharist liturgy known technically and casually as the offertory. Here we need to see clearly the implications and amplifications of our participation in Christ's sacrifice. I want to make three observations in this connection.

The offertory is the time of the preparation for the Great Thanksgiving which it initiates, the gathering and presentation of alms and the presentation of bread and wine. Given the fact, as we have said above, that the priesthood that is being acted out with these things is the priesthood of the church, it seems wisest to me for these things to be put in place by those who gather (the alms) and make (bread and/or wine) them. Further, I would argue that these same people might very well remain at the altar/ table during the prayer of blessing and even assist in the distribution of the bread and wine at communion. Sadly, the rubrics seem unsympathetic to this suggestion.

Secondly, even though Gordon Lathrop is obviously right in saying that we Christians do not literally make sacrifice, given talk of altars and given that we carry "gifts" to them, there is something of the "look" of a sacrificial event, even to those for whom the theological idea of sacrifice would be unattractive. In the form of our alms and bread and wine carried through the congregation as is our custom, the people standing, and in the metaphorical sense on which we have relied earlier, we can "see" *ourselves* being carried to a place of sacrifice, there to be made holy, surrendered, there to pass over into God's own possession. And in that this is so for ourselves, we can "see" that it is so also for all of creation. What a compelling moment this might be, when rightly "seen," a moment compelling thanksgiving and engagement in the life of the world.

Thirdly on this matter, there needs to be about our offering of substantial things and ourselves a serious and severe modesty, however joyfully we may approach it. Though unintended by Christians in the developed west, there is an arrogance about our offering processions that can be seen with clarity by those who view our parades of food and money from a place of hunger and want. Our offering is made hypocritical if what we give is exhausted by our own use, our own maintenance and continuance, our own well-being. Our action of offering is made less hypocritical if what we give is "sacrificed" for the good of the world, used *imitatio Christi*, in the imitation of One who saved others but could not save himself.

I am coming more and more to believe that the principal rationale for the gathering of alms and their presentation in the public liturgy can only be that we must perform a ritual action whose meaning has the potential to form and direct us. It is the ethical power implicit in our offertory action that is its rationale, not the raising of funds.

Before concluding this chapter, it seems wise to say a word or two about the object that typically rests in the most prominent place in the liturgical room, often the "east" end, kept to itself by rails, its typical companions being candles and cloth, perhaps flowers.

In the first of Thomas Cranmer's two Prayer Books, this object was called an "altar." That was the word used in the received tradition. In the second Prayer Book, this conservative word was abandoned in favor of "table" (and "God's board"). Choosing between altar and table was necessary in his time for politico-theological reasons—Cranmer's favorite kind of reason. In our time, however, it seems unnecessary to choose, and so the current revision of the American Prayer Book uses both, in rubrics and prayer texts alike. By using both names, the Prayer Book sets loose the constellations of images associated with each, thereby complicating and enriching the theology it teaches and implicitly laying aside the necessity to choose.

I wish, therefore, that in common parlance we would begin to call this central eucharistic object an "altar/table" and in so doing habituate the church to the theological nuances this combination suggests. To the extent that calling it an "altar" or "table" relates to old high church/low church struggles, the combination would liberate both parties. And to those who know nothing of these sometimes arcane debates, the double name simply conveys a more abundant truth than either by itself.

Elsewhere, I have made suggestions as to where the altar/table ought to stand, relative to the assembly and relative to the place of preaching and reading (a place where the mutuality and reciprocity of altar/table and ambo are evident).[14] Similarly, the history of the altar/table can be traced elsewhere.[15] The contours of such a history would move from commonplace wooden table in daily domestic use, to special table, to stone surface in a burial place, to stone altars containing either saint or relic or sacrament, to stone objects appearing to be sarcophagi, to moveable wooden tables removed when not in use, to fixed stone altars fronted or surrounded by high rails then lower ones, to whatever one finds in our time. So it goes. What draws our attention now is the matter of where one who offers, stands.

Given my suggestions that altar/table be the way we speak of the object in question, a suggestion intended not only to name the object rightly but also, thereby, to avoid having to make an unnecessary choice, I want now to suggest that the presider's "place to stand" be treated similarly. That is, if we "read" an eastward facing posture as altar-related (priest facing the same direction as the congregation), and a westward facing posture as table-related (priest facing toward the congregation), these two postures could be used in the same room on different occasions, varying by seasons or some other suitable guide.[16] As the double name would send its proper signals, so also would the variable posture, seen and explored over time. Varying the place of the priest, relative to the congregation, would certainly invite enquiry and provide a fruitful opportunity for teaching.

In our talk of offering and sacrifice, we must continuously remind ourselves that the sacrifice which we offer, that is the sacrifice in which we participate, is offered for the sake of the world. It is not for ourselves only that we make our appeals to God, but rather, and more importantly, for the sake of the world of which we are a part, a world for which the one sacrifice was made, full, perfect and sufficient, once upon a time.

---

1. The thoughtful reader will have discovered long ago that I myself am not particularly pleased with the survival of "priest" as the name for presbyters in the church. That the word lingers, however, lays upon people like me the obligation to use it, especially since it is so common a part of the received liturgical and canonical vocabulary for the Episcopal Church. (My future holds, I hope, an exploration of a particular expression of this idea, namely, "sacred priesthood," as it is put in the rite for priestly ordination. The question I want to pursue is in what lies the sacrality of "priesthood" vis-a-vis the baptized?)

2. *Accept This Offering: The Eucharist as Sacrifice Today* (Collegeville, MN: The Liturgical Press, 1989). Those interested in exploring the full set of objections can refer to Stevenson and his larger work on the same subject, *Eucharist and Offering* (New York: Pueblo, 1986).

3. *Ibid.*, p. 2.

4. *Ibid.*, p. 4.

5. *Holy Things*, cited earlier, p. 140.

6. *Ibid.*, p. 142.

7. (Philadelphia: Fortress, 1978), p. 140.

8. *Ibid.*

9. *Visible Words: The Interpretation and Practice of Christian Sacraments* (Philadelphia: Fortress, 1978), pp. 63–64.

10. *The Collected Poems of Howard Nemerov* (Chicago: University of Chicago Press, 1977), p. 441.

11. I am indebted to comments in David Power's *Unsearchable Riches*, cited earlier, pp. 154ff for some of what follows. My exposition, however, is somewhat different.

12. James Agee and Walker Evans, *Let Us Now Praise Famous Men* (Boston: Houghton Mifflin, 1941), p. 15.

13. See for example David L. Balas, *Metousia Theou: Man's Participation in God's Perfections according to Saint Gregory of Nyssa*, Studia Anselmiana 55 (Rome: Pontifical Institute of S. Anselm/Herder, 1966) for a treatment of our theme and its elaboration through the fourth century.

14. See "Preaching and the Potential of Liturgical Space" in *Breaking the Word*, edited by Carl Daw (New York: Church Hymnal, 1994).

15. For a good, quick review see C.E. Pocknee, "Altar" in *The New Westminster Dictionary of Liturgy and Worship*, edited by J.G. Davies (Philadelphia: Westminster, 1986), pp. 6–8.

16. See my article "An Apology for Variable Liturgical Space," *Worship*, 61/3 (May, 1987).

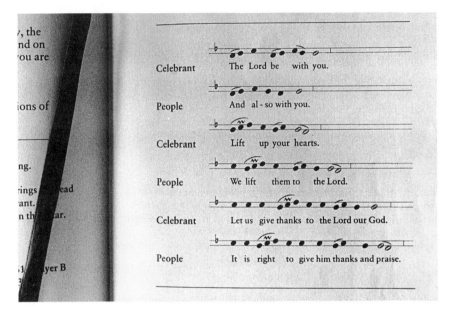

ONE WHO SPEAKS

We have passed through six images to this point and in each instance the apparent association has been between the image at hand and the eucharist understood in association with the altar/table. It is time we addressed this association, broadened it and thereby set it right.

The Prayer Book teaches clearly that the Holy Eucharist is composed of two integral parts, the Word of God and Holy Communion as the text names them. This way of speaking testifies to the mutuality and interdependence of the parts and argues directly against any suggestion that the eucharist and the altar/table liturgy are to be equated. We come then in consequence to consider the presider and the care of words, including the Word, and the speaking of them.

Obviously, prior to this point, we have talked about words, and equally obviously, one who presides is not the only one who speaks (or listens) in the liturgy. Yet, along with the other images that fill this book, it is surely appropriate and timely for us to spend some time and energy on the speaking done by the presider and the reading and hearing done in the liturgical gathering.

As a beginning, consider these words by Howard Nemerov. The poet gives us "The Makers," words about words and their coming to be, and he gives us good theology.

Who can remember back to the first poets,
The greatest ones, greater even than Orpheus?
No one has remembered that far back
Or now considers, among the artifacts
And bones and cantilevered inference
The past is made of, those first and greatest poets,
So lofty and disdainful of renown
They left us not a name to know them by.

They were the ones that in whatever tongue
Worded the world, that were the first to say
Star, water, stone, that said the visible
And made it bring invisibles to view
In wind and time and change, and in the mind
Itself that minded the hitherto idiot world
And spoke the speechless world and sang the towers
Of the city into the astonished sky.

They were the first great listeners, attuned
To interval, relationship, and scale,
The first to say above, beneath, beyond,
Conjurors with love, death, sleep, with bread and wine,
Who having uttered vanished from the world
Leaving no memory but the marvelous
Magical elements, the breathing shapes
And stops of breath we build our Babels of.[1]

Speaking within the assembly is perhaps the most easily identified responsibility taken on by the priest in a liturgical community. As people with a deep fondness for books (the Bible and the Book of Common Prayer), Episcopalians gather around words. (This fact raises serious challenges in settings in which literacy cannot be taken for granted. It also is a fact that carries dynamic justice issues as literacy becomes a way of including or excluding people.) It is the presider's remarkable obligation to convene the community, to call the Body of Christ to attention with words of acclamation and blessing. And from this beginning through moments of edification, thanksgiving and communion, the words spoken by the presider (though not "the presider's words") serve as a continuous thread upon which the liturgical texts are strung.

Given the preoccupation of the biblical tradition with words and their power, and the power associated with one who speaks, the presider ought to approach the invitation to speak with due reverence, humility, preparation and care. The words that the presider is privileged to speak are words of extraordinary power, words which, in the company of equally powerful actions, accomplish what they say. Things and people who receive words (and actions) of blessing are blessed, words (and actions) of forgiveness affect forgiveness, words (and actions) intending transformation actually transform. The priest in the liturgy speaks words that change things and people.

As we explore the liturgy's words, I am moved to admit a certain double-mindedness. Earlier we talked a good deal about the priority of actions to words in the liturgy. I confessed to a suspicion that the actions are the source of power, touching something in us and in the cosmos below and before the point of engagement for words. The words then become their companions, descant, sometime exegete. Yet it is nonetheless true that the words are the more easily read, the more "legible" form of commerce among us and their influence, even power, is undeniable. Much as I may wish that the physicality and gestural beauty of, say, dance were the most edifying and rewarding form of communication in the human community, I quickly admit the greater weight, in our time and society, possessed by "sound bites" and "factoids."

The reading and preaching of the Word is the central business of the first part of the eucharistic liturgy. In most places it is the presider who is the gospeler and the preacher, and either directly or by example, the teacher of liturgical reading in most congregations. This being so, it seems appropriate for us to consider this dynamic work in the current context.

As to preaching, clearly we cannot undertake an extended discussion of the complex subject in this place. And, for that matter, I would be well advised to leave a reasoned discussion to wiser heads than mine.[2] I would simply like to wish and suggest that preachers preach expecting something to happen, expecting that whatever they imagine to be the gracious consequence of bread and wine eaten and drunk, would also occur by the hearing of the Word read and proclaimed. I would pray that preachers expect that from preaching would come strength as well as solace, renewal as well as pardon; that by this preaching our eyes would be able "to see [God's] hand at work in the world about us"; and that the grace of the Word richly and faithfully proclaimed would "make us one body, one spirit in Christ, that we may worthily serve the world in his name."[3] To hope and claim such for (sacramental) preaching is no more extravagant than to claim such for (sacramental) eating and drinking.

As to the reading of the Bible, it seems imperative that this be done with utmost care, preparation and expectation. I am frequently dismayed by the lack of attention paid to public reading and the failure to understand the impact of its being well or badly done. Indeed, since the introduction of those little inserts in the Sunday bulletin, the ones on which the readings are printed, public reading seems to have degenerated even more. The Bible is intended to be heard, not read! More accurately, the Bible intends to be *told*, and so it came to be.

Reading in church would be so much better, in my view, if we suppressed those little inserts until after the liturgy was over, offering them to people who wanted to take them home for further reflection, meaning people who did not own a Bible I suppose. For the reading of the Bible in the liturgy, we ought to require that readers read as if edification depended upon them, and that hearers be taught to attend to the readings as if something powerful were to be revealed there. We ought also, when we read the Bible, to *read from the Bible* (and a proper formal Bible at that) and not from something else. The "bookness" of the Bible (biblos) is part of the deal!

As to the readings themselves, I offer several comments. First, in the eucharistic liturgy there is a hierarchy of readings, reinforced by a similar hierarchy of readers. This is not true when the same readings occur in the

Daily Office. In the eucharist, the Gospel must be read by an ordained person (except in "Rite III") whereas in the Office there is no such stipulation. The sequence of the readings is also fixed in what appears to be a pattern rooted in a hierarchical assumption. In addition, in many congregations, efforts are made to accord to the reading of the Gospel special ceremonial attention, peculiar to this particular reading, viz., the Gospel procession.

The relationship between the public reading of the Bible and preaching is an intimate one and must be. This is the reason that preaching follows immediately upon the readings and the reason the Prayer Book, in the eucharistic liturgy, invites absolutely nothing in between. Given this intimacy, and given the fact that preachers often preach on a text other than the gospel appointed, one wonders about the virtue of the fixed sequence of the readings. Why not read just before the sermon the reading upon which the sermon is based? This seems to make the most ritual sense and would create a recognizable continuity for the hearers.

An anecdote will serve by way of illustration. At a meeting of the North American Academy of Liturgy some years ago, in the majestic Gothic "chapel" at Duke University, an evening eucharist was celebrated, attended by liturgy "experts" from across the continent. There were three readings. The first two were read from a modest lectern by first a man and then a women, dressed in what my sister-in-law calls "good casual clothes." Following the second reading, the reading from the apostle Paul, the presider (who was also the preacher), accompanied by torches and preceded by a thurifer, ascended the pulpit, censed the Bible, read from the Gospel, and, having focused the assembly's attention on that reading then preached on the first reading, the one from the Old Testament. This made ritual nonsense! If we are going to single out one of the readings for special attention or status (something we Episcopalians do not do in the Office), what would have made sense would have been giving ritual dignity to the reading on which the preacher was to expound and for it to be read just before the sermon. (However much sense this suggestion makes, and it makes a good deal to me, the rubrics with which we live will not permit it.)

This discussion raises for me yet another matter, namely the popular custom of processing the Gospel. This practice, intended as I understand it to give "ritual dignity" to a particular reading, often strikes me as ill conceived and incongruous given this intent. More often than not, a procession in the midst of which is borne the gospelbook or Bible travels from an elevated and well lighted place where the acoustics are generally good into a poorly lighted place with no elevation and poor acoustics—and all this in order to give "ritual dignity." The practice of processing the Gospel used to be a procession to an elevated place, a place of greater dignity, on the way to which was sung a psalm from a step (*gradus* hence gradual). Our efforts to read the Gospel "from the midst of the people," if a proper motivation, is really a judgment on the buildings in which the Gospel is read. If the liturgical space were set right, the reading of the Gospel (and the rest of the Bible as well) would naturally occur "in the midst of the people."

We turn now to the voice of one who speaks and the speaking. The instrument used by the presider to render liturgical words is his or her own natural voice, used in a public mode without affectation or pretense. (Only the British are entitled to British accents!) And since the liturgy, in whatever setting, is always "formal," meaning that the liturgy is always public and corporate, the voicing of the language of the liturgy is necessarily "solemn."

Referring to the word "solemn," Dan Stevick has written, "The word now usually means doleful, stiff, and austere. In its older sense, solemnity was not incompatible with joy, festivity, and celebration. The solemn thing was simply a thing whose idiom was unlike the casual, the conversational, or the ordinary. Behind the idiom was the sense that some things and some moments were of such largeness of meaning that they required an expression in something other than the familiar, everyday style."[4] Stevick goes on to say, "When 'solemnity' was still a cultural possibility, a person taking part in a ceremony or speaking with dignity and richness of style was not being self-important; he was obeying the inner, expressive logic of the ordered occasion. His role was within an understood context. C.S. Lewis once commented in this connection: 'The modern habit of doing ceremonial things unceremoniously is no proof of humility; rather it proves the offender's inability to forget himself in the rite, and his readiness to spoil for everyone else the proper pleasure of ritual.'"[5]

In addition, the voice of one who speaks must be heard. Each word or line given to the presider is to be heard clearly and said with respect, including "let us pray" and other such formulaic material. In the liturgy, there are no "throwaway lines." In order to see that this is so, one who speaks needs always to be "in place" before speaking, except when in procession. Speaking in a ritual context while moving should be limited to those processional moments in which the cadence of the words seems to take cognizance of the rhythm of footfalls, the Great Litany for example or the opening anthems of the Burial Office.

There is an oddity of evolution in one of the texts the presider says most commonly. I refer to the greeting, "The Lord be with you" and what, to my mind, is the curious way it is typically said.

Most often we hear these words said in a way that apparently derives from the Latin for the same words, *Dominus vobiscum*. In the Latin, the middle syllable of the second word receives the accent. When this pattern is transferred to English, we get, "The Lord be *with* you," which seems odd to me. (It seems to invite a response similarly accented, "And also *with* you.") More sensible would be almost any other rendering. For example, "The *Lord* be with you," or "The Lord *be* with you," or—and this seems best to me—"The Lord be with *you*." To this last would come the meaningful reply, "And also with *you*." I have no way of discovering the evolution of the most frequently heard pattern but, for my part, I would like to see it abandoned in favor of some other. What we say ought to make sense.

To extend this point a bit further, one who speaks in the liturgy ought always to voice the liturgical texts in such a way as to reveal their sense. How many times have any of us heard prayer texts read in a flat and "senseless" fashion, reminiscent of a time when liturgical "recitation" was taken to be the heart of liturgical work. Those days are gone, happily. At the same time, the vitality with which the texts should be read for meaning should not be replaced by histrionics, an equally "senseless" approach, or worse, by sentimentality.

In several places throughout these chapters, I have made reference to the presider's need for continuous assistance and continued training and reflection upon the work of liturgical leadership, both within and without the liturgy. As regards the voice of one who speaks, most of us have available to us valuable and informed assistance. This help grows out of the competence of good church musicians. The choir director or organist in a congregation can often provide useful insight and give sound advice to the priest about the use of the voice, projection, elocution and breathing, and all to the good of the church's liturgy. Seeking such help and advice would not only assist the priest's continuing liturgical education but would likely assist in fostering an appropriate relationship between the presider and the musician, a relationship that sometimes needs more tending than it gets.

The obvious companion to speaking in the liturgy is *not* speaking in the liturgy. In Howard Nemerov's poem "The Makers," cited earlier, the poet observed that those who "worded the world . . . were the first great listeners."[6] Would that it were so with those who, presiding, speak. The way this concern would express itself in the liturgy would be for the presider to honor the silences, to engage them with patience and expectancy, and to assist the assembly in so doing.

Silence-keeping as a formal and ordered part of the liturgy is a particular gift of the current revision of the Prayer Book. Silences which found their way into the liturgy during the tenure of previous editions arrived there as a consequence of error—someone forgot something or the like. The current revision has taken with more seriousness the necessary rhythm of speaking and not speaking. In keeping this rhythm we are granted permission to wait, listen, be silent together, and, if it may be, to be still. Those who preside in the liturgy ought not to neglect these occasions and by neglecting deprive the assembly of a wonderful and perhaps elsewhere unexpected moment. I find myself thinking that the silences are like gesture and movement in their ability to reveal and need to be "expressed" with care and respect. The keeping of the silences also runs contrary to our cultural penchant for pragmatism and efficiency, and that seems quite a healthy thing as well. (Robert Hovda noted that the liturgy always "has maintained its subtle but relentless witness against the facts of life."[7] Silence-keeping is such a witness.)

The rhythm of speaking and silence-keeping is established in order to showforth the integrity (wholeness) of the liturgy, its balance and its imitation of the pattern of language itself and its participation in the cadence of human life. The interconnectedness and reciprocity of all this is conveyed by something T.S. Eliot said about a "phrase or sentence that is right

(where every word is at home,
Taking its place to support the others,
The word neither diffident nor ostentatious,
An easy commerce of the old and the new,
The common word exact without vulgarity,
The formal word precise but not pedantic,
The complete consort dancing together) . . ."[8]

It may seem ironic to use Eliot's words about words to suggest something about speaking and not speaking but perhaps the point is made rightly nonetheless. What I am after is to suggest something about the "complete consort dancing together," in which one who presides takes the lead.

On page 14 of the Prayer Book, near the end of those rubrics gathered under the heading "Concerning the Service of the Church," one finds the following, "Where rubrics indicate that a part of the service is to be 'said,' it must be understood to include 'or sung,' and *vice versa*." Although I have built this chapter about words around the notion of one who speaks, I would rather have built around another notion, namely, one who sings.

I wish it were true that we understood the liturgy to be a thing rightly sung and only "said" under unusual circumstances. I wish we recognized that the music of the liturgy was not an addition or ornament but was, rather, endemic to it, the one constitutive of the other.

A story is told of an Austin architect who had just completed the construction of a new building in Houston when a hurricane hit that city. He called Houston to learn the status of the new building. Someone at the site, in answer to the architect's query about the health of the building, said, "Well, the building's fine but some of the architecture blew off." The analogy here is to the presider unable to see the intimate interconnectedness of liturgy and music (architecture and building).

If we were to take seriously the appropriateness and necessity of music to the liturgy, it would place upon the presider the necessity of singing, and the ability to do so. Among the Orthodox, as I understand it, such ability is prerequisite to ordination. Among us it ought to be. I say this knowing that for some this is an alienating suggestion and to others an impossibility, but as principle it stands. Further, my hunch is that if more priests possessed more musical gifts and musical sensibilities, the character of our understanding of priesthood (and liturgical life) would change, and to the good.

The words of the liturgy, the words of reading and proclamation are central to the faithful expression of our life with God. The presider, as one who speaks (sings) them in the midst of the assembly, is blessed by doing so.

To conclude this chapter, consider a few words about things unscripted, "non-liturgical" words often spoken by one who presides. These words are the Announcements and the announcements.

The announcements are almost always unnecessary, at least for the normal Sunday liturgy. Between the bulletin, the hymnboard and the regular congregation, there is no reason why the presider should have to provide incidental notices. Doing so, though some would argue it is related to hospitality, I would argue is related to the clericalization of the liturgy. If, however, there arises some unexpected need, whatever is said should announce whatever is needed in the most economical fashion, calling as little attention as possible to the presider's own person.

As to Announcements, these, like the Peace, have a way of overpowering the liturgy, becoming in this case something like a town meeting. To my mind, the place for such speaking is *before* the liturgy begins, meaning before the entrance hymn. Made at such times, liturgical information for the day can be shared, strangers can be welcomed, whatever there is that needs to be passed along can be handled with dispatch. In addition, and very importantly, music for the day can be introduced, taught and learned. A good musician can teach new music sufficiently well in a very short time for it to be well sung in its rightful place later on. This is the easiest way I know to develop the singing of the congregation, continuously aided by the choir.

Such things being done at the outset, the Announcements having been accomplished, the liturgy can move at its proper pace without intrusion. The Body of Christ can gather itself and give itself over to the praise and enjoyment of God.

1. In *Sentences* (Chicago: University of Chicago Press, 1980), p. 65.

2. I should call the reader's attention to the following sources: *Breaking the Word,* edited by Carl Daw, cited earlier; Paul Marshall, *Preaching for Today's Church* (New York: Church Hymnal, 1990); Tom Troeger, *Imagining a Sermon* (Nashville: Abingdon, 1990); and Patricia Wilson-Kastner, *Imagery for Preaching* (Minneapolis: Fortress, 1989). As I mentioned in the preceding chapter, I have a chapter in the Daw book, exploring the relationship of preaching and liturgical space.

3. See Eucharistic Prayer C, BCP 1979, p. 372.

4. *Language in Worship,* cited earlier, p. 171.

5. Ibid., p. 172.

6. *Sentences* (Chicago: University of Chicago Press, 1980), p. 65.

7. *Strong, Loving and Wise,* cited earlier, p. 21.

8. "Little Gidding," V, *The Complete Poems and Plays, 1909–1950* (New York: Harcourt, Brace and World, 1971), p. 144.

ONE WHO CELEBRATES

The procession of images brings us back to where the Prayer Book terminology would have had us begin, one who celebrates, celebrant. In an earlier place (chapter on "One who Presides"), we talked about the inappropriateness of this designation for the priest, given the fact that the liturgical room is filled (one hopes) with "celebrants," thus making unsuitable such a name for just one of them. In that same place, however, we were forced to admit that given the Prayer Book's use of the term, we were stuck with it. And being "stuck" we will happily explore it to conclude, though surely not complete, these reflections on the shaping of the ministry of presiding in the liturgical community.

It has been true for years that in casual church parlance, one who was to preside at the church's eucharist was called "the celebrant." It was not until the current revision of the Prayer Book, however, that the title found its way into the rubrics. In fact, in the trial-use texts that paved the way for the 1979 Prayer Book, beginning with "The Liturgy for the Lord's Supper" in 1967 through the texts available in "Authorized Services" of 1973, the one who was to preside was called "the priest," the rubrical title most common in our tradition, "the minister" being second best. Between the 1973 trial-use texts and the first passage by General Convention of the "new" Prayer Book in 1976, "celebrant" replaced "priest." And so we have it for our exploration.

As I have pondered the treatment of this image, I find a strange yet delightful thing happening. I find that it is with this image that the heart and mind want release to flights of imagination, permission to traverse lines of academic propriety and explore the further, perhaps more exotic informants of liturgical leadership. In granting myself such release and permission, and notifying the reader of such, we move to consider play, clowns and dressing up, the blessings and complexities of festivity. (The tendency toward extravagance which visits me as I contemplate the current topic is also shared by those whom I will gather to assist in this exploration.)

Over seventy years ago, in the years before the current rush of liturgical revisions, well before the warmth provided to the Roman Catholic Church (and the rest of us) by the energy of John XXIII and the Second Vatican Council, Romano Guardini wrote *The Spirit of the Liturgy*.[1] There is a beauty, almost a grandeur in Guardini's writing that most would envy.

Of special note is his chapter entitled "The Playfulness of the Liturgy." Something of the spirit of the entire book and this particular chapter is conveyed by the tone of the first sentence, "Grave and earnest people, who make the knowledge of truth their whole aim, see moral problems in everything, and seek for a definite purpose everywhere, tend to experience a peculiar difficulty where the liturgy is concerned."[2] As one often beset by "grave and earnest people," Guardini has me on his side from the opening gambit and on to the very end.

Guardini strives to set the categories "purpose" and "meaning" side by side and argue that, for the liturgy, there is meaning but (external to itself) no purpose. "Purpose," he writes, "is the goal of all effort, labour and organisation, meaning is the essence of existence, of flourishing, ripening life."[3] To invoke "purpose" as a category for evaluation of the liturgy is inappropriate, Guardini says, in the same sense that it would be inappropriate to use "purpose" to assess the work of an artist or the play of a child.

The author writes so gloriously I must let him speak without paraphrase: "The child, when it plays, does not aim at anything. It has no purpose. It does not want to do anything but to exercise its youthful powers, pour forth its life in an aimless series of movements, words and actions, and by this to develop and to realize itself more fully; all of which is purposeless, but full of meaning . . . And because it does not aim at anything in particular, because it streams unbroken and spontaneously forth, its utterance will be harmonious, its form clear and fine; its expression will of itself become picture and dance, rhyme, melody and song. That is what play means . . ."[4]

". . . picture and dance, rhyme, melody and song." How marvelous to be able to see this, not only in play but in the liturgy! The liturgy, he says, "has no purpose, but it is full of profound meaning. It is not work, but play. To be at play . . . is the essence of the liturgy."[5]

At the conclusion of his chapter, Guardini puts a marvelous spin on the self-consciously "didactic aim" to which some (the purposeful ones) would want to put the liturgy. "It is in this very aspect of the liturgy (its being like play or art) that its didactic aim is to be found, that of teaching the soul not to see purposes everywhere, not to be too conscious of the end it wishes to attain, not to be desirous of being over clever and grown-up, but to understand simplicity in life. The soul must learn to abandon, at least in prayer, the restlessness of purposeful activity; it must learn to waste time for the sake of God, and to be prepared for the sacred game . . . It must learn not to be continually yearning to *do* something, to attack something, to accomplish something useful, but to play the divinely ordained game of the liturgy in liberty and beauty and holy joy before God."[6]

What an extraordinary vision! To play "in liberty and beauty and holy joy before God."

Whatever the pragmatism of Guardini's time, surely ours is possessed of more. Yet even in this time of ours, one who celebrates the saving sacraments of the church must have, kept safe in a deep and accessible place, a comparable notion, something that sets loose the heart, that animates the fluids that nourish the body, that brings to the "clever and grown-up" side of oneself the visceral recollection of what it is like to play.

I could wish few finer gifts on one who celebrates than the full grasp of this vision. To know in one's heart that in the liturgy we are, as Louis Weil has called us, "player(s) before God."[7]

Then, having visited this gift upon one who celebrates, I would be quick to point out, as Guardini does in his own fashion, that play does not lack discipline or order. It is not aimless or meandering, any more than the play of a child. In fact, as any parent will attest, the playful constructs of children are redolent with more order than most of the rest of life after childhood. This is why the play of children is such a splendid metaphor for the church's eucharistic celebration, holding together as it does the freedom of the outpouring of the playing itself and the order which allows it to be shared and to continue to exist.

The luxurious view which Guardini offers here has proven prickly and uncomfortable to some. These are quick to point out that in the liturgy, as in play, things are in fact accomplished, as if with purpose. That social, sacramental and ritual things are accomplished is undeniable, as I hope to have made clear throughout the previous pages. At the same time, and this is very important to grasp, I would argue that the *purpose* which the church pursues in the liturgy is contained within the liturgy itself and is not external to it. Speaking analogously, it is clearly true that the play of children provides an occasion for the development of social skills, dexterity and coordination, imagination and self-understanding but it seems highly unlikely that this is the *reason* or *purpose* resident in the mind of the children who play. They are *playing*. (I can just imagine a child asking, "Mommie, may I *please, please, please* go over to Sally's to work on socialization and my fine motor skills?")

In the gathering of the liturgical community and in their celebration of the saving acts of God in Christ, much is accomplished, largely by way of God's generosity towards us. But what we intend is what the liturgy intends and nothing more. As with the play of children, these ancillary benefits of our "play," however strong they may be, come to us as grace.

To my mind, there is a good deal of energy in the idea of "play" which transfers itself easily to the idea of "liturgy." To the extent that this transfer is appropriate, it should alert one who presides to the physical and emotional consequences of liturgical leadership. The involvement of the body in this work ("play") is considerable and should be. Like most forms of play, it is embodied, animated, visceral, and requires and expends energy. And, like most games in which the body is fully engaged, the players need proper physical preparation, sustenance and rest.

However "extravagant" one may find Guardini's insights about the liturgy and play, what we move to now will push the settled imagination even further. To "play" we add the clown.

As anthropologists would teach us, societies "need" the benefit of social paradox and contradiction. The person who acts out this need is called by various names, trickster, jester, fool, clown.

Kenneth Feit called this person "the priestly fool" in an essay by that name, written twenty years ago.[8] Though he can be rightly charged with confusing the analytical categories "priest" and "shaman" as we (and others) have used them earlier, his exploration of "the priestly aspect of folly" rewards our attention. The confusion to which I point is manifest and made entirely forgivable in the following definitional statement: "The term 'priest' is used here genetically to describe that person, male or female, who is a discerner of wonder, mystery, and paradox: who celebrates life and death; who is a story-teller and listener; who is a focuser of community (though frequently living on the periphery of the community); who is a proclaimer of the truth (verbally and non-verbally); who is a servant and healer of the poor (powerless); and who resymbolizes, reritualizes, and remythologizes for the tribe."[9]

This is quite a description! And there is more to come. But before going on, and in order to dispense with them quickly, I need to say two things. Feit's definition is a provocative and excessive definition, one that needs to be appropriated for what it evokes but without being put on as if a suit of clothes intended to be a good fit. What Feit is talking about, as he makes clear as his article unfolds, is really a description of gifts rather than skills, things "native" rather than learned. Insofar as this is so, most of those who preside will not be in full possession of them, some not even close.

A second mild caveat is to say that Feit's description of the fool as a liturgical figure fixes too exclusively on the person of the priest to the neglect of others, making the work or ministry, if you will, of the clown too heroic and privately specific, given the social and communal nature of the liturgy itself and the fact that the "priestliness" is that of the community.

Now, having demurred slightly, I want very much to promote serious consideration of the texture or ethos implicit in Feit's view, taking with greatest seriousness the suggestion of eccentricity. The work [play] given to one who celebrates is genuinely odd, as surely the line of images we have explored suggests. (I have discovered its "oddness" even more as I have tried to describe to people distant from the presider's work (play) what it is that I am writing this book about. By most societal tests, this is odd stuff!)

In the person of the clown, Feit finds expressed the character of the one Aristotle called *eutrapelos*, the "grave-merry master."[10] Anyone who knows the circus even a little will recognize this figure. (Those of a certain age will quickly see the classic face of Emmet Kelly.) As an image alive for Christian theology, the clown becomes a Christlike figure. What makes the clown so apposite in this regard is the "kenosis" by which a clown becomes a clown. By this self emptying, "the clown loses sexual identity, becoming neither male nor female, but assuming the guise of one or both (hence the many transsexual circus gags of male clowns in dresses wearing balloons). The clown also loses . . . personal history and is ageless, being neither old nor young but transcending time. As such the clown belongs to no race or cultural grouping, but lives on the edge of all societies, defying containment by law, mores, and reason."[11]

Central to the persona of the clown, of course, is whiteface, the disguise and definitional "vesture" of clowning. Once "vested" with whiteface, the kenosis is signaled and becomes the only alternative. "In whiteface, the clown may not use his ordinary voice; he must remain silent or exaggerate his voice. He may not eat, drink, or smoke unless it has a comic effect . . . Once made up, the clown may not eliminate or make love, nor may he feel pain . . . Ultimately the clown may not even die since he is always expected to bounce back buoyantly from each mishap. The specter of a clown seriously injured from a fall or mauling, lying helplessly in the center ring, is almost sacrilegious . . . The principal celebrant (of the 'liturgy of wonder') must forfeit tongue, stomach, lungs, bladder, genitals, nerve endings, even his psychic identity and the power to end the sacrifice by ritual death." [12]

Surely this exceeds anything incumbent upon one who presides in the gathering of the baptized but in its excess it is nonetheless evocative of certain realities, luring one who celebrates into the consideration of new and challenging notions.

And although mime is not the metier of one who presides, the putting-on of vesture is. Feit writes, ". . . the artful, playful, and sacred share a common domain. Art, play, and prayer are the only human activities that are totally purposeless yet absolutely meaningful (unlike work which is thoroughly purposeful and usually meaningless). Thus the fool and priest join the artist in a conspiracy of meaning. May they learn well each other's song and dance and wear a common motley." [13]

When the clown puts on his or her face, the jester his or her motley, the priest his or her liturgical vesture, it marks a decisive moment of entry into both concealment and disclosure. Here we touch a matter of direct importance to the church's liturgical life and identity.

In an essay called "Liturgical Vesture in the Roman Catholic Tradition" in Chrisa C. Mayer-Thurman's *Raiment for the Lord's Service*, Aidan Kavanaugh suggests that the *"function* of liturgical vestments is said to be twofold: to act as insignia designating the diversity of liturgical ministries, and to contribute to the dignity of the rite itself." [14] In the library copy of this book which I have used, an earlier insightful reader quite irresponsibly penciled the following addition to Kavanaugh's definition: "and to give universal commonality rather than individual identity." It seems to me that the writer who should not have written in this book makes a genuine and important contribution, actually offering what might have been said first.

As with whiteface and motley, so also with ritual vesture. One who takes these on takes on the anonymity associated with any uniform and the disclosure of meanings which such uniforms gather to themselves and set loose. And with liturgical vesture, particularly eucharistic vesture, the meanings gathered and let loose are those of the liturgical community and not those idiosyncratic to the priest. Here is, perhaps, where our analogies break down.

What Feit says about the clown, fool, jester, however evocative of meaning for one who celebrates, must not "fool" us into thinking that the priest's liturgical work (play) is privately held or privately owned. The ritual event is the event of the community and the symbols set in motion "belong" to the community. The festival is the festival of Christ's Body.

This means, in my view, that the central eucharistic garment, the chasuble, should not be privately held or owned by one who presides, but should rather be the festal garment of the community and understood by all to be such.[15] This being so, in vesting for the celebration of the church's eucharist, one who celebrates drapes about oneself the "fabric" of the community in the midst of which one is privileged to stand. And so vested, one testifies to one's servanthood and anonymity while signaling and showingforth the "grave-merry," death-resurrection texture of the church's self-understanding.

Further, following this line of reasoning, the festal garment's residency in the community means that it will survive the priestly tenure of many. Indeed, in those rare instances of multiple priests in a given place, the community's festal garment (or garments if such be the case for seasonal reasons) will adorn the backs of each in turn.

The beauty of this understanding is that each who wears the garment participates in the lineage of the church in that place and can, in a matter of speaking, take residency in the garment as a place of safety and comfort "in spite of oneself." Let me explain, and likely risk misunderstanding.

To the extent that vesture is a uniform it is also a disguise. For many priests, this latter is a true blessing. It is a blessing in the same way that a pall over a casket is a blessing. Like the pall, the chasuble provides us a character of like kind with others, without regard to our private sins and weaknesses, not even reliant on our presumed strengths. In Angela Carter's *Nights at the Circus* to which I referred earlier (in note 12), the principal clown, Buffo the Great, now in a vodka induced melancholy, says, "Under these impenetrable disguises of wet white, you might find, were you to look . . . the *aerialiste* whose nerve has failed; the bare-back rider who took one tumble too many; the juggler whose hands shake so, from drink or sorrow, that he can no longer keep his balls in the air."[16] In each instance, however, as Buffo makes plain, the clown's "reality," sustained and expressed by whiteface, holds and protects.

This talk of palls and failure should not lead the reader to a sorrowing conclusion about my view of presiding—the misunderstanding which I feared in citing this example. Instead, the reader should simply recognize the character and appropriate extent of the anonymity our liturgical "disguise" affords, and being aware, acknowledge it and be glad.

Now, having made much of the wearing of vesture, I want to turn our discussion a bit and to wonder out loud, as it were, about the appropriateness of associating the festival colors, to cite the most obvious example, only with the presider (and presumably other symbolbearing aspects of the liturgical "furniture"). To make my point, I offer a telling incident. It is common on ordination invitations for the following line to appear: "Clergy, red stoles." This is predictable and useful information. At a recent such event, however, a modest but significant change was made. Instead of sending everyone on the mailing list information intended only for some, everyone on the mailing list was given information relevant to themselves. That is, instead of the usual ("Clergy, red stoles"), the invitation simply said, "The festival color is red." This small change brought about a wonderful result at the ordination itself. In addition to red stoles on priestly (and diaconal) shoulders, others in attendance were set out in red hats, coats, shirts or blouses, shoes, handbags, scarves, ties, some even reported wearing red examples of clothing not typically visible in public. In other words, the festival color expressed itself much more richly than the former "clerical" information ever achieved. This modest change did wonders to enhance the festive air of the event and did equal good to soften the excessive clerical "feel" of this most clerical of the church's liturgical offerings.[17]

As to the nature of liturgical vestments, I should say very little, save the following. Frank Kacmarcik, the preeminent liturgical design consultant of this generation in the Roman Catholic Church, rarely passes a chance to rail against the habit of some of "putting symbols on symbols."[18] (I am persuaded of his argument.) As I have heard his tirades more than once, it is typically about baptismal fonts that he expresses concern. But surely the same truth can be applied to liturgical vesture. It ought to be the garment itself, its material and color that constitutes its "meaning," which is obviously complex and multivalent. This inherent richness ought to be allowed to speak its own piece without its having to bear the burden of something sentimental or didactic intended to "explain." Even worse, turning the eucharistic vestment into a billboard for "religious" slogans ought surely to be avoided.

This is, perhaps, enough about play, clowns and dressing-up. Before concluding this chapter, something more needs to be said about music.

By any self-respecting definition, a celebration is a musical event. In an earlier chapter, I have suggested as much already. This means that chief among the celebrants are the musicians and those who lead them. This also means that one ought to have to show cause why *not* to sing (or dance) the liturgy rather than the other way round.

This seems particularly true in at least one special instance. Even in the most austere and meager circumstances, in the presence of the smallest gathering with the giving of the most spare gifts, at no time during a birthday celebration would those in attendance honor the birthday-person by *saying*, "Happy Birthday to you, Happy Birthday to you, Happy Birthday, dear Methuselah, Happy Birthday to you." Similarly, at what New Year's Eve celebration, amidst hats, horns, streamers, champagne, chaos, resolutions and tears, would the assembly *say*, "Should old acquaintance be forgot and never brought to mind. . . ."? Neither of these would happen, even if both occasions were populated by people who could not find a pitch with a map and a flashlight, or carry a tune in a washtub. Why then, one wonders, does the song of the angels in the liturgy get *said* in any celebration of the eucharist? If we admitted that in the *Sanctus* we were in fact joining "with angels and archangels and all the company of heaven," then surely whatever poverty our singing exhibited would be more than carried by the celestial harmonies. And think how pleased the angels would be and how honored God, were we to sing this melody sweetly! In any case, sing we must.

The eucharist which the church celebrates we know to be a foretaste of a much grander meal, an hors d'oeuvre and aperitif announcing the Messianic Banquet, whetting our appetites for more divine victuals. The Prophet has told us about it,

On this mountain the LORD of hosts will make for all peoples
   a feast of rich food, a feast of well-aged wines,
   of rich food filled with marrow, of well-aged wines strained clear.
And he will destroy on this mountain
   the shroud that is cast over all peoples,
   the sheet that is spread over all nations;
   he will swallow up death forever.
Then the Lord GOD will wipe away the tears from all faces,
   and the disgrace of his people he will take away from all the
   earth,
   for the LORD has spoken.
It will be said on that day,
   Lo, this is our God; we have waited for him, so that he might
   save us.
   This is the LORD for whom we have waited;
   Let us be glad and rejoice in his salvation
                        (Isaiah 25:6–9, NRSV).

It is to this prospect and this promise that we respond, "Celebremos la fiesta!" From me, then, bon appetit . . .

---

1. Translated by Ada Lane (London: Sheed and Ward, 1930). It was originally published in 1922.

2. *Ibid.*, p. 85.

3. *Ibid.*, p. 92.

4. *Ibid.*, pp. 98–99.

5. *Ibid.*, p. 102.

6. *Ibid.*, pp. 105–106.

7. "The Christian as Player before God," *Nashotah Review*, Spring, 1974.

8. *Anglican Theological Review*, Supplementary Series Number Five (June, 1975).

9. *Ibid.*, p. 97.

10. *Ibid.*, p. 104.

11. *Ibid.*, p. 105.

12. *Ibid.* In Angela Carter's novel *Nights at the Circus*, there is an extraordinary speech made by the chief clown in Colonel Kearney's circus, Buffo the Great. It is filled with delicious pathos and sadly much too long to rehearse here. I cannot, however, forswear the following still rather too long portion. In it, the sodden Buffo says:

> 'There is a story told of me, even of me, the Great Buffo, as it has been told of every Clown since the invention of the desolating profession,' intoned Buffo . . .
>
> 'In Copenhagen, once, I had the news of the death of my adored mother, by telegram, the very morning on which I buried my dearly beloved wife who had passed away whilst bringing stillborn into the world the only son that ever sprang from my loins, if "spring" be not too sprightly a word for the way his reluctant meat came skulking out of her womb before she gave up the ghost. All those I loved wiped out at one fell swoop! And still at matinee time in the Tivoli, I tumbled in the ring and how the punters bust a gut to see. Seized by inconsolable grief, I cry: "The sky is full of blood!" And they laughed all the more. How droll you are, with the tears on your cheeks! In mufti, in mourning, in some low bar between performances, the jolly barmaid says: "I say, old fellow, what a long face! I know what *you* need. Go along to the Tivoli and take a look at Buffo the Great. He'll soon bring your smiles back!"
>
> 'The clown may be the source of mirth, but—who shall make the clown laugh?'
>
> (New York: Penguin, 1993 [1984]), pp. 120–121.

13. *Ibid.*, p. 108. The author is an obvious benefactor of the insights of Guardini.

14. *Raiment for the Lord's Service: A Thousand Years of Western Vestments* (Chicago: The Art Institute of Chicago, 1975), p. 13.

15. Kavanaugh rightly says that the eucharistic vestment "is a garment, not a costume." *Ibid.*, p. 14. I am content, however, as he might not be, to call it a uniform.

16. Cited earlier, p. 119.

17. The ordination to the priesthood of Amy Donohue and Betsy Ungermann, St. Francis' Church, Houston, Diocese of Texas, March 14, 1994.

18. I have heard Br. Frank's views pungently expressed on a nearly annual basis in the Environment and Art Study Group of the North American Academy of Liturgy, of which he and I are a part. He is a Benedictine Oblate.

Epilogue

As a teacher, part of my professional life and ministry is given over to pointing out to others places where joy, edification, satisfaction and stimulation can be found. To however great an extent I myself must provide these blessings, it is the more necessary for me to direct students and others elsewhere, beyond myself, to find these rewards. In this way, teaching is the art of introduction.

In some measure this is what I have tried to accomplish in these chapters, to introduce the reader to sources and ideas, both my own and those of others, in the hope that from these introductions formation might occur. It is surely true that the list of images I have chosen and explored could be altered or extended. (Paul James, for example, writing in England very recently, suggests that the liturgical president is a person who welcomes, arranges, acts with authority and is a person of prayer[1]) But for the sake of some measure of economy, I have settled on the eight images into which we have looked.

In the Preface to the preceding chapters, I suggested that teachers of liturgy need to function both as *conservators* of the church's liturgical tradition and its conventional assumptions and expectations regarding one who presides, and as *provocateurs* of that tradition's "most creative expression and enrichment." I also expressed the hope that those who read these pages would adopt the same view towards themselves and their use of these ideas. I reiterate that invitation here.

It is, in my view, particularly with the provocateurs that the church's liturgical health resides. Much of what I have proposed which may come to some readers as novelty is, in fact, simply the expression of what exists in the current rubrics. It is flexibility and not innovation that they discover. At the same time, there are points of view which are not commonly held and suggestions which exceed current bounds. I am bold enough to hope that these suggestions will find a home in the life and practice of the church's liturgy in the same way so many other things have, namely, by coming into use prior to, yet in anticipation of, rubrical permission. We are, after all, a church committed to order on the basis of custom not rules, a fact which gives our liturgical life a folkloric character, rubrics not withstanding. It is into that "customary" pattern of change that I want to insinuate whatever "irregular" views one may find contained here.

It is my habit, at the beginning of school each fall, to distribute to all my students a list of practical liturgical directives called "Small Things."[2] Named such because it contains such, the same name might appear as the title of this book. Since it is the accumulation of small things which gather to constitute the church's liturgical life and practice, it is with small things that one who presides must contend.

This is all the more necessary because what we do in the liturgy *is* our theology, embodied, enlivened, incarnated. Our praise of God ("doxology") is our doctrine of God ("theology"). The *ecclesia* we see and know in the liturgy expresses and teaches us how we are to understand the church, how the Body of Christ works (plays), how the ministry of the Risen One is to be acted out in the world. Surely, this makes our attention to small things, collected together, very important.

Benedictus es.

---

1. *Liturgical Presidency* (Bramcote, Notts, UK: Grove, 1993), pp. 48–49.

2. The title is taken from remarks made by Thomas Cranmer in his treatise "Of Ceremonies" which accompanied the first Book of Common Prayer, 1549.